nickelodeon™

降 击 神 通

AVATAR

THE LAST AIRBENDER™

Created by
Bryan Konietzko
Michael Dante DiMartino

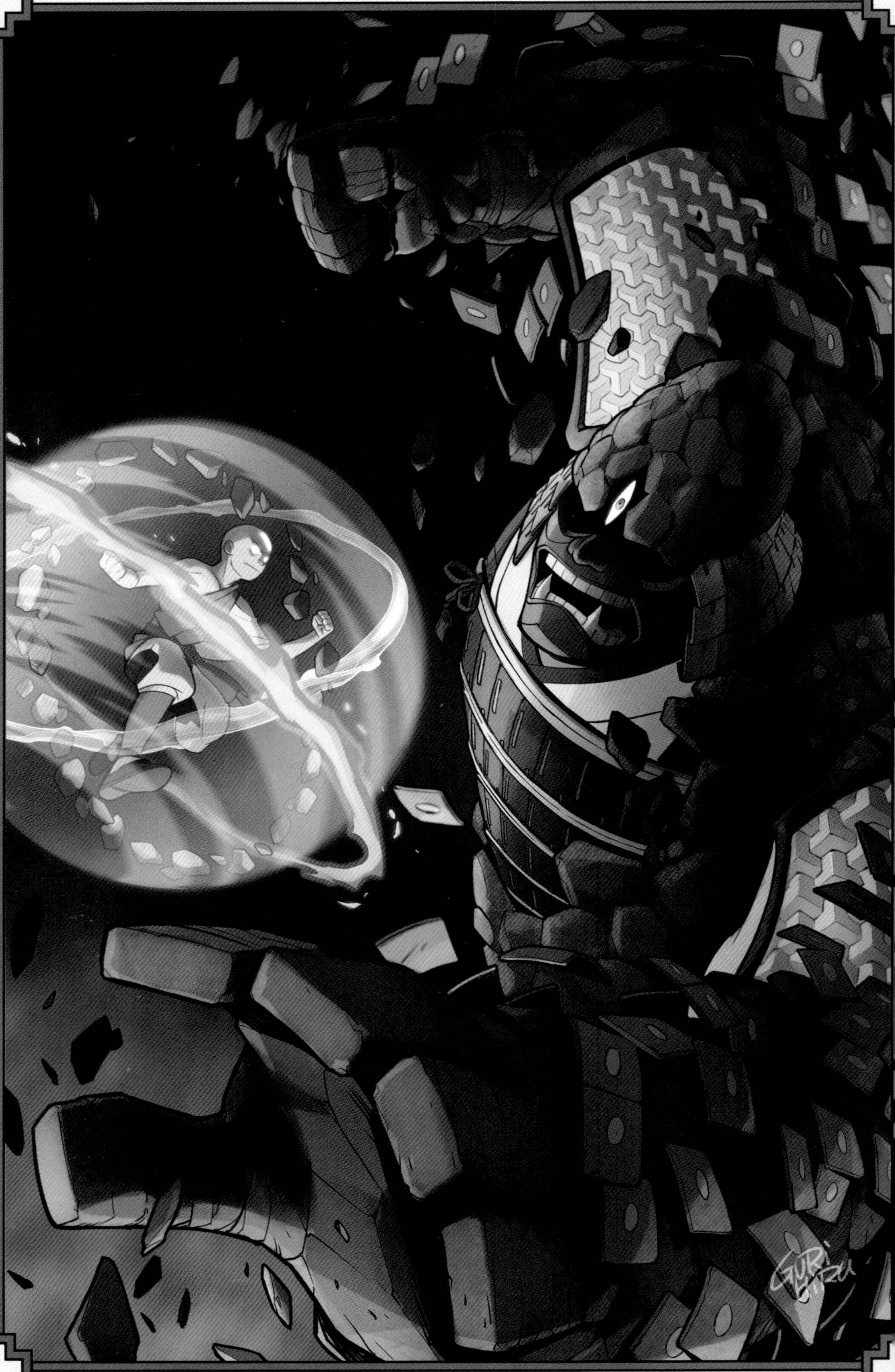
GURI HIRU

nickelodeon

降击神通

AVATAR

THE LAST AIRBENDER

THE RIFT · PART THREE

script
GENE LUEN YANG

art and cover
GURIHIRU

lettering
MICHAEL HEISLER

DARK HORSE BOOKS

president and publisher
MIKE RICHARDSON

collection designer
JUSTIN COUCH

assistant editors
ROXY POLK and **AARON WALKER**

editor
DAVE MARSHALL

Special thanks to Linda Lee, Kat van Dam, James Salerno, and Joan Hilty
at Nickelodeon, and to Bryan Konietzko and Michael Dante DiMartino.

Published by **Dark Horse Books**
A division of Dark Horse Comics, Inc.
10956 SE Main Street, Milwaukie, OR 97222

DarkHorse.com
Nick.com

International Licensing: (503) 905-2377
Comic Shop Locator Service: (888) 266-4226

First edition: November 2014 | ISBN 978-1-61655-297-8

1 3 5 7 9 10 8 6 4 2
Printed in China

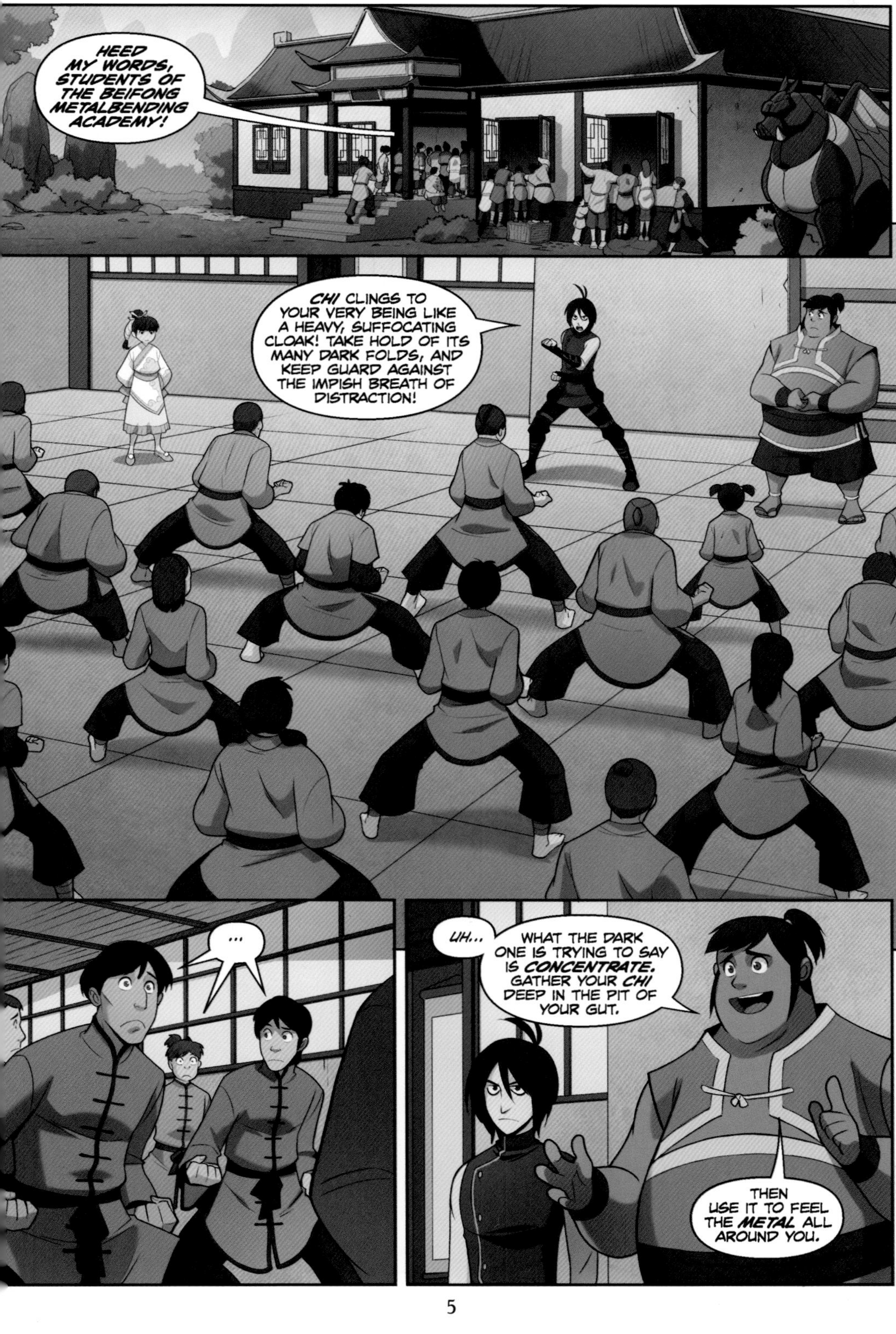
HEED MY WORDS, STUDENTS OF THE BEIFONG METALBENDING ACADEMY!
CHI CLINGS TO YOUR VERY BEING LIKE A HEAVY, SUFFOCATING CLOAK! TAKE HOLD OF ITS MANY DARK FOLDS, AND KEEP GUARD AGAINST THE IMPISH BREATH OF DISTRACTION!
...
UH...
WHAT THE DARK ONE IS TRYING TO SAY IS CONCENTRATE. GATHER YOUR CHI DEEP IN THE PIT OF YOUR GUT.
THEN USE IT TO FEEL THE METAL ALL AROUND YOU.

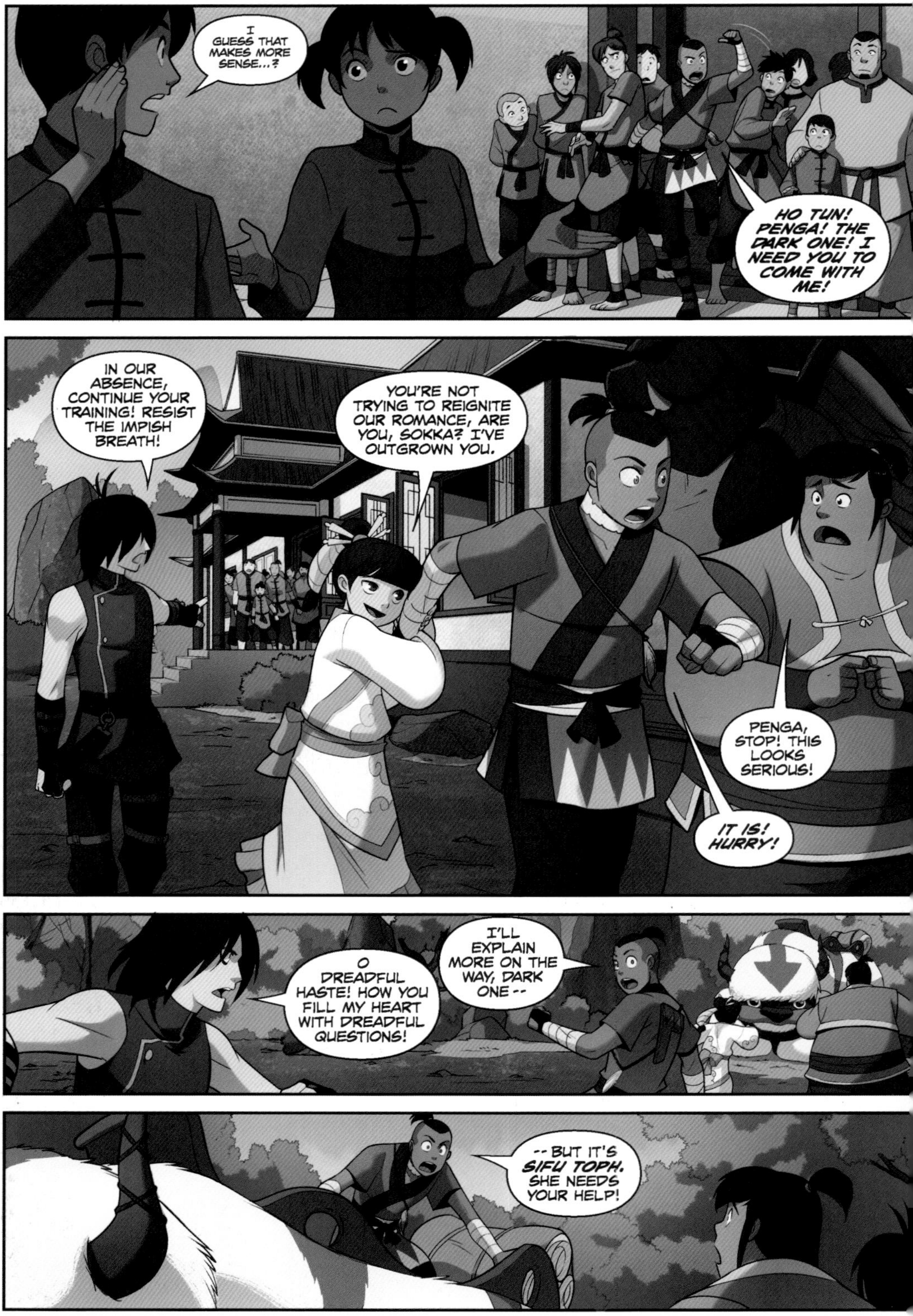
I GUESS THAT MAKES MORE SENSE...?
HO TUN! PENGA! THE DARK ONE! I NEED YOU TO COME WITH ME!
IN OUR ABSENCE, CONTINUE YOUR TRAINING! RESIST THE IMPISH BREATH!
YOU'RE NOT TRYING TO REIGNITE OUR ROMANCE, ARE YOU, SOKKA? I'VE OUTGROWN YOU.
PENGA, STOP! THIS LOOKS SERIOUS!
IT IS! HURRY!
O DREADFUL HASTE! HOW YOU FILL MY HEART WITH DREADFUL QUESTIONS!
I'LL EXPLAIN MORE ON THE WAY, DARK ONE --
-- BUT IT'S SIFU TOPH. SHE NEEDS YOUR HELP!

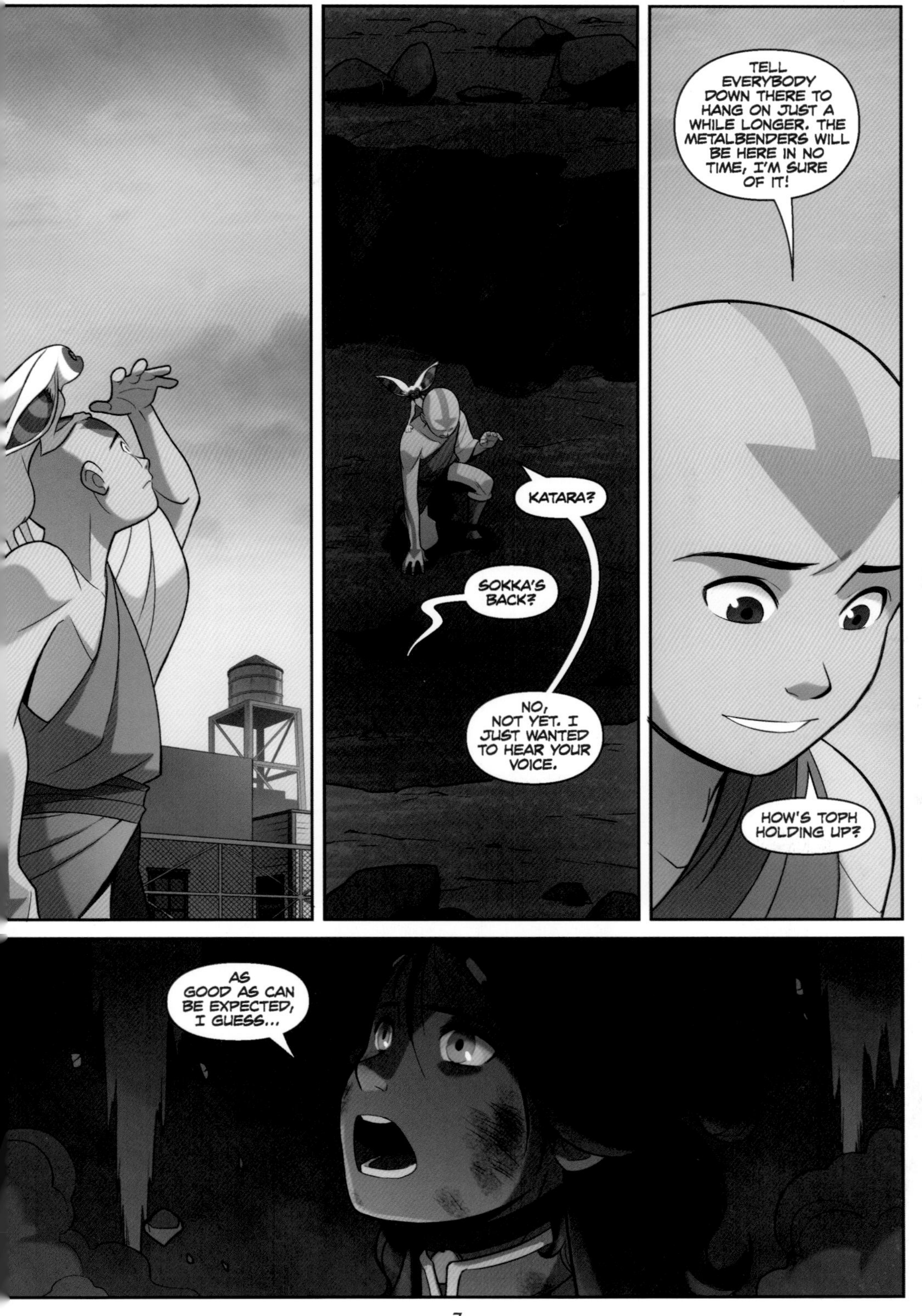
KATARA?
SOKKA'S BACK?
NO, NOT YET. I JUST WANTED TO HEAR YOUR VOICE.
TELL EVERYBODY DOWN THERE TO HANG ON JUST A WHILE LONGER. THE METALBENDERS WILL BE HERE IN NO TIME, I'M SURE OF IT!
HOW'S TOPH HOLDING UP?
AS GOOD AS CAN BE EXPECTED, I GUESS...

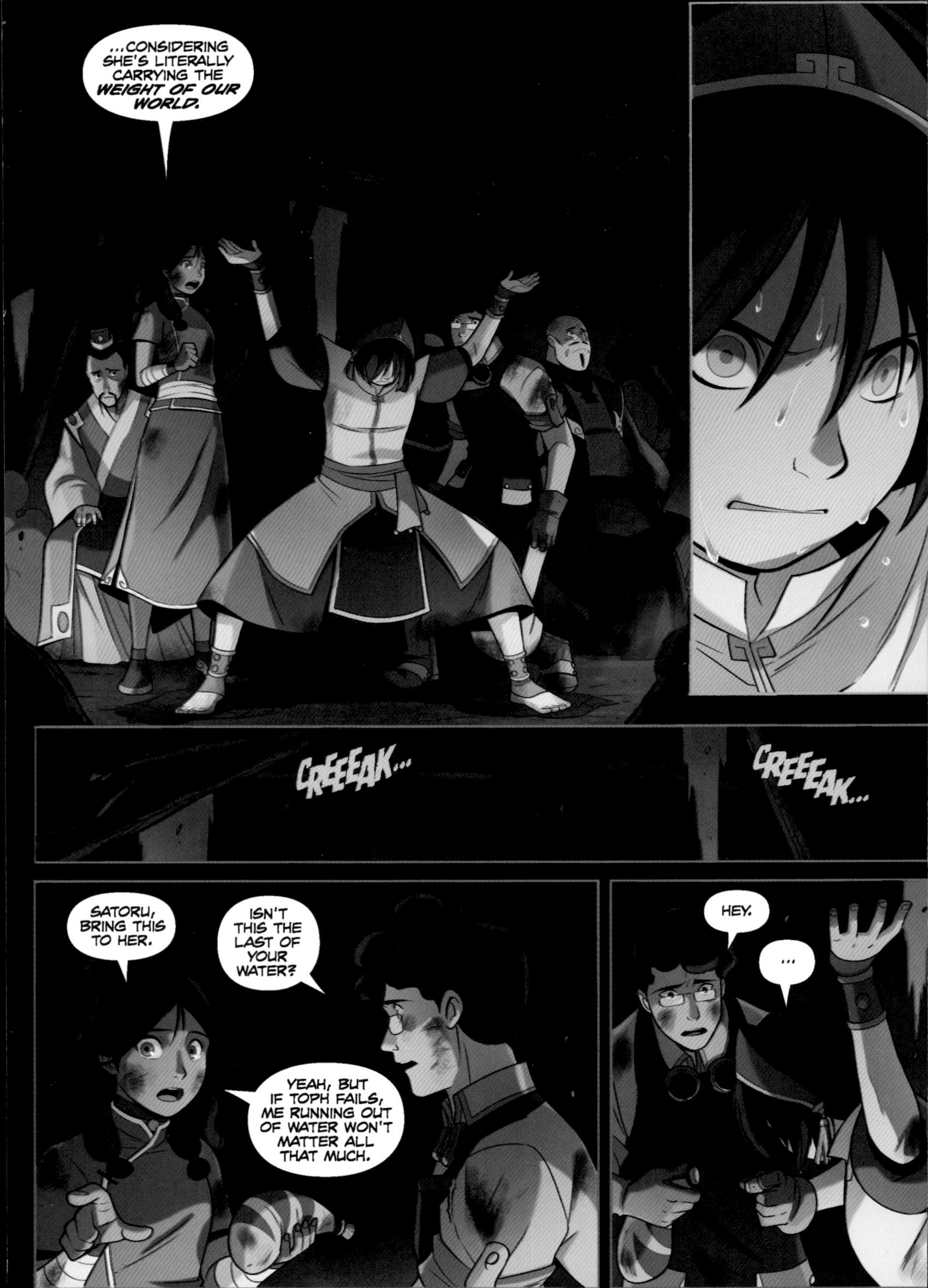
...CONSIDERING SHE'S LITERALLY CARRYING THE *WEIGHT OF OUR WORLD.*
CREEEAK...
CREEEAK...
SATORU, BRING THIS TO HER.
ISN'T THIS THE LAST OF YOUR WATER?
YEAH, BUT IF TOPH FAILS, ME RUNNING OUT OF WATER WON'T MATTER ALL THAT MUCH.
HEY.
...

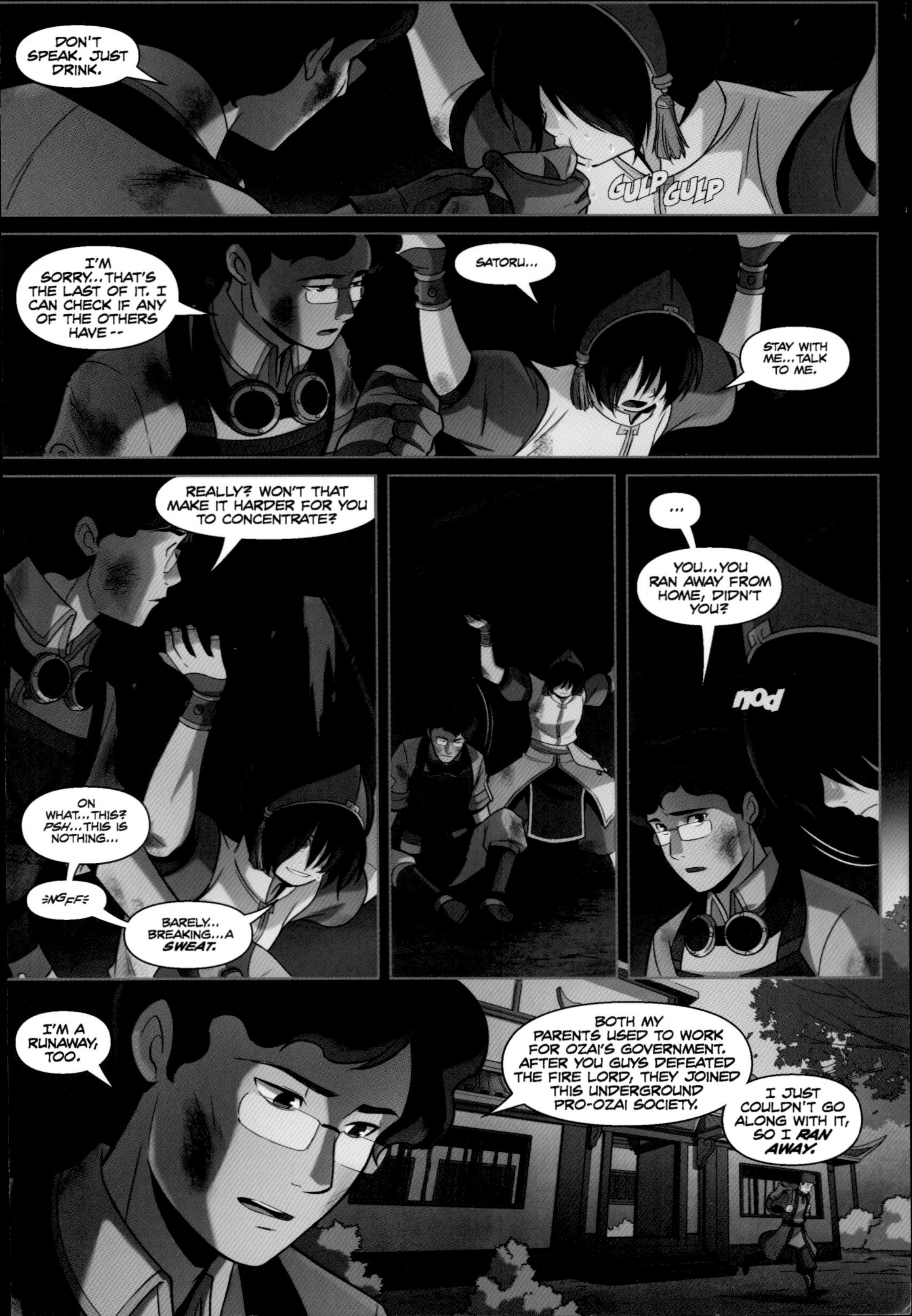
DON'T SPEAK. JUST DRINK.
GULP GULP
I'M SORRY...THAT'S THE LAST OF IT. I CAN CHECK IF ANY OF THE OTHERS HAVE --
SATORU...
STAY WITH ME...TALK TO ME.
REALLY? WON'T THAT MAKE IT HARDER FOR YOU TO CONCENTRATE?
ON WHAT...THIS? PSH...THIS IS NOTHING...
≥NGFF≤
BARELY... BREAKING...A SWEAT.
...
YOU...YOU RAN AWAY FROM HOME, DIDN'T YOU?
nod
I'M A RUNAWAY, TOO.
BOTH MY PARENTS USED TO WORK FOR OZAI'S GOVERNMENT. AFTER YOU GUYS DEFEATED THE FIRE LORD, THEY JOINED THIS UNDERGROUND PRO-OZAI SOCIETY.
I JUST COULDN'T GO ALONG WITH IT, SO I RAN AWAY.

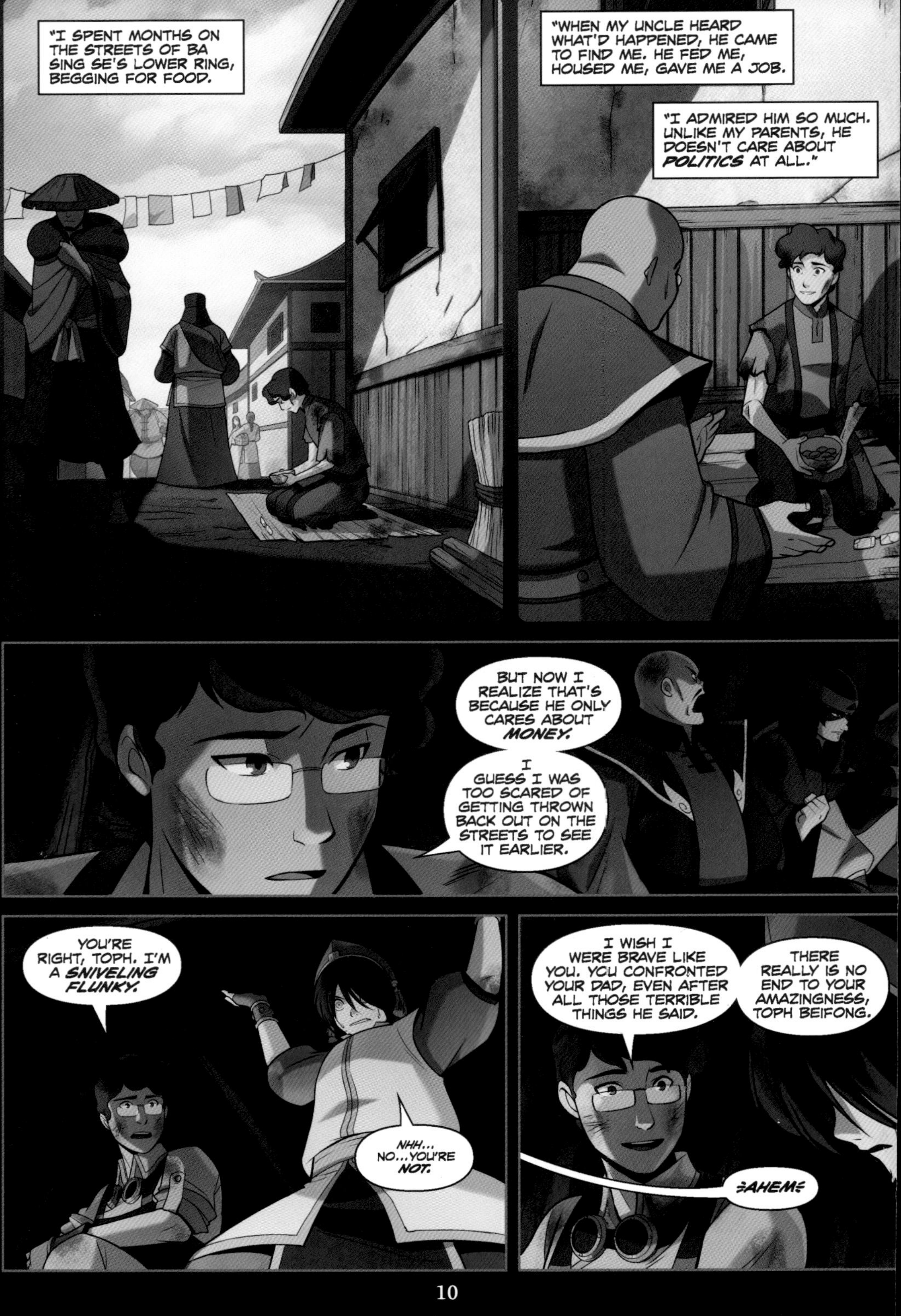
"I SPENT MONTHS ON THE STREETS OF BA SING SE'S LOWER RING, BEGGING FOR FOOD.
"WHEN MY UNCLE HEARD WHAT'D HAPPENED, HE CAME TO FIND ME. HE FED ME, HOUSED ME, GAVE ME A JOB.
"I ADMIRED HIM SO MUCH. UNLIKE MY PARENTS, HE DOESN'T CARE ABOUT *POLITICS* AT ALL."
BUT NOW I REALIZE THAT'S BECAUSE HE ONLY CARES ABOUT *MONEY.*
I GUESS I WAS TOO SCARED OF GETTING THROWN BACK OUT ON THE STREETS TO SEE IT EARLIER.
YOU'RE RIGHT, TOPH. I'M A *SNIVELING FLUNKY.*
NHH... NO...YOU'RE *NOT.*
I WISH I WERE BRAVE LIKE YOU. YOU CONFRONTED YOUR DAD, EVEN AFTER ALL THOSE TERRIBLE THINGS HE SAID.
THERE REALLY IS NO END TO YOUR AMAZINGNESS, TOPH BEIFONG.
AHEM

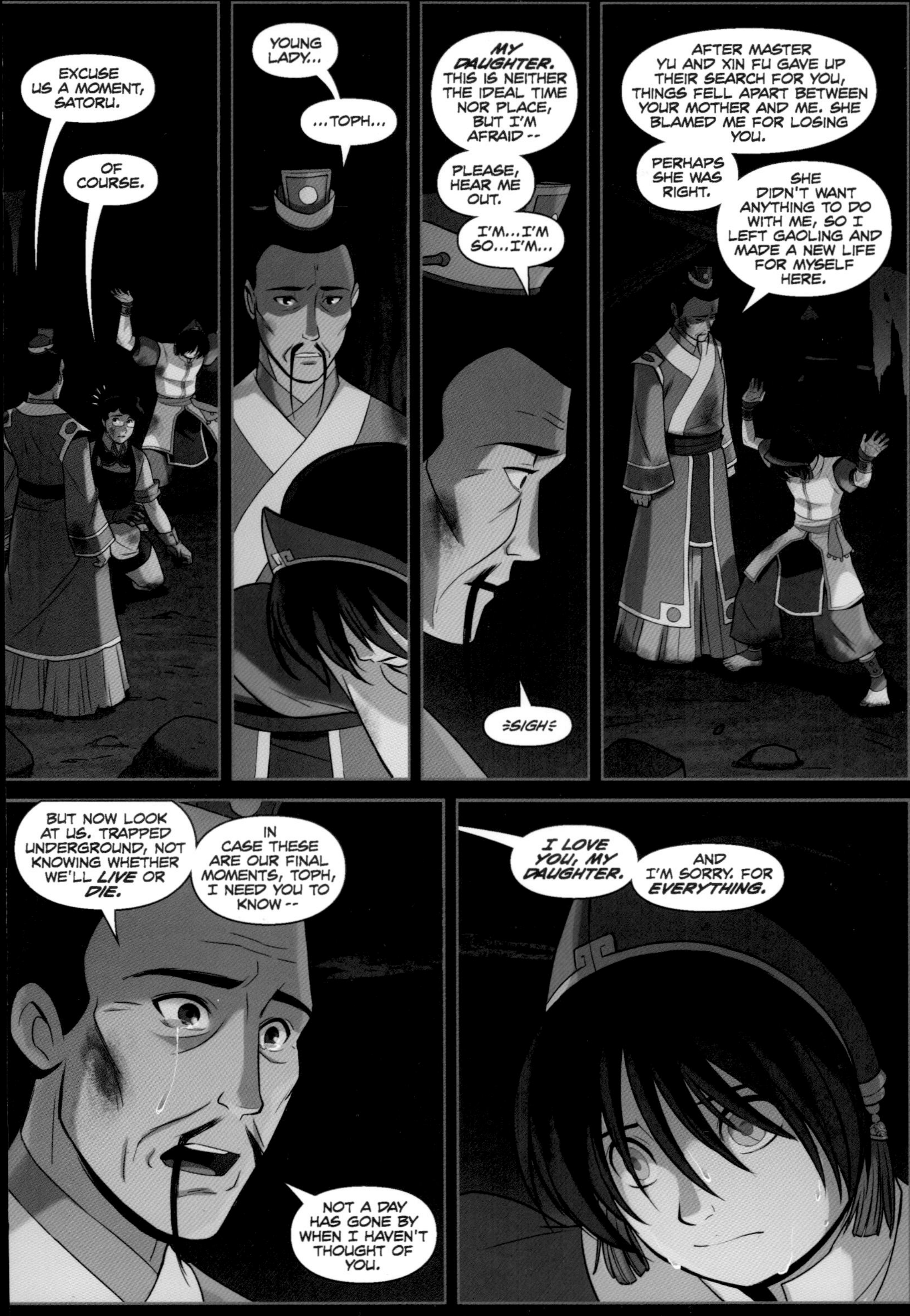
EXCUSE US A MOMENT, SATORU.
OF COURSE.
YOUNG LADY...
...TOPH...
MY DAUGHTER. THIS IS NEITHER THE IDEAL TIME NOR PLACE, BUT I'M AFRAID --
PLEASE, HEAR ME OUT.
I'M...I'M SO...I'M...
≶SIGH≶
AFTER MASTER YU AND XIN FU GAVE UP THEIR SEARCH FOR YOU, THINGS FELL APART BETWEEN YOUR MOTHER AND ME. SHE BLAMED ME FOR LOSING YOU.
PERHAPS SHE WAS RIGHT.
SHE DIDN'T WANT ANYTHING TO DO WITH ME, SO I LEFT GAOLING AND MADE A NEW LIFE FOR MYSELF HERE.
BUT NOW LOOK AT US. TRAPPED UNDERGROUND, NOT KNOWING WHETHER WE'LL *LIVE* OR *DIE.*
IN CASE THESE ARE OUR FINAL MOMENTS, TOPH, I NEED YOU TO KNOW --
NOT A DAY HAS GONE BY WHEN I HAVEN'T THOUGHT OF YOU.
I LOVE YOU, MY DAUGHTER.
AND I'M SORRY. FOR *EVERYTHING.*

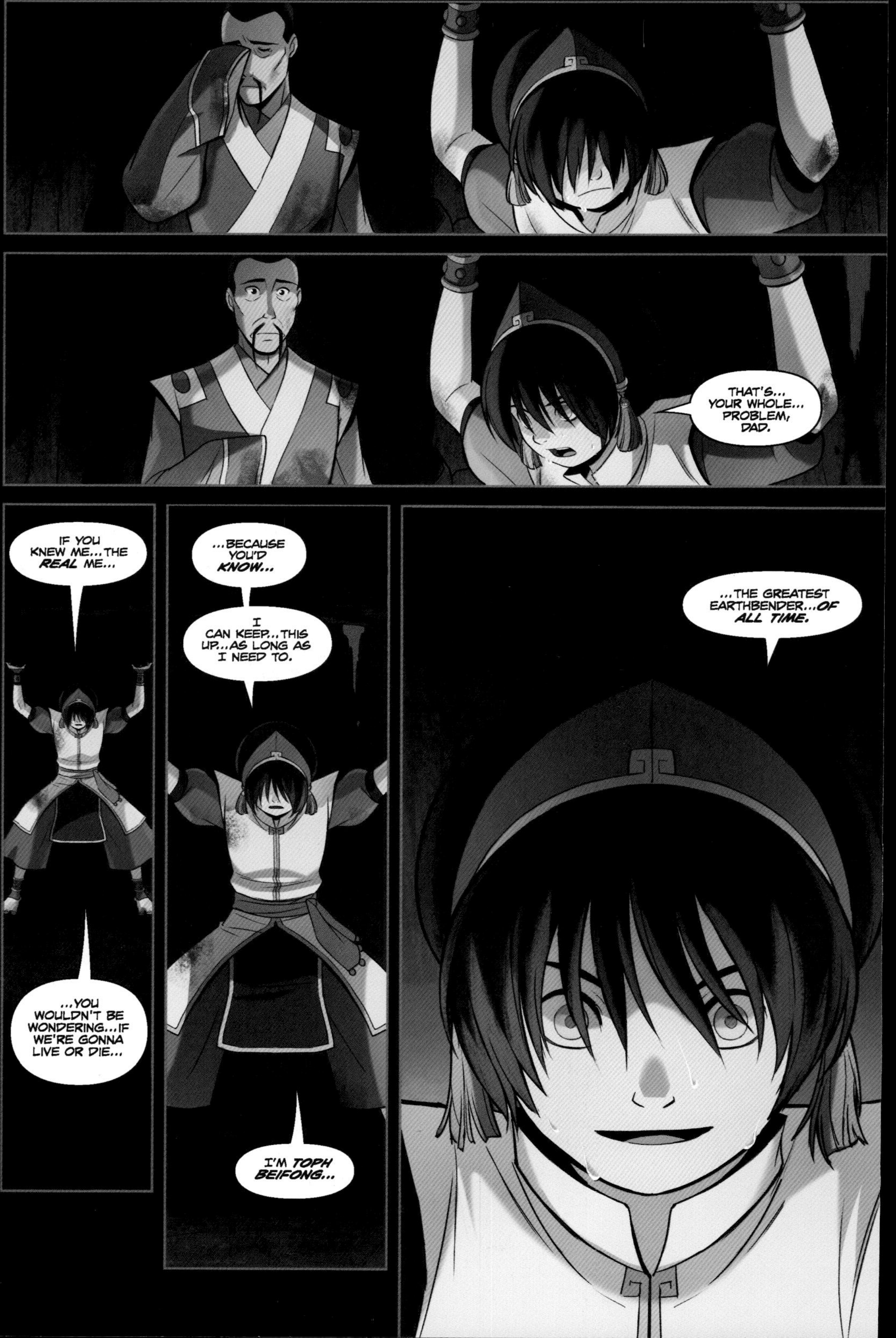
THAT'S... YOUR WHOLE... PROBLEM, DAD.
IF YOU KNEW ME... THE REAL ME...
...YOU WOULDN'T BE WONDERING... IF WE'RE GONNA LIVE OR DIE...
...BECAUSE YOU'D KNOW...
I CAN KEEP... THIS UP... AS LONG AS I NEED TO.
I'M TOPH BEIFONG...
...THE GREATEST EARTHBENDER... OF ALL TIME.

KATARA! THEY'RE HERE! TOPH'S STUDENTS ARE HERE!

THAT'S WONDERFUL! I'LL GO TELL TOPH!

METALBENDERS! ARE WE GLAD TO SEE YOU GUYS!

SIFU TOPH AND A BUNCH OF OTHER PEOPLE ARE BURIED UNDERGROUND, IN A COLLAPSED MINE! I CAN'T DIG THEM OUT BECAUSE THEY'RE UNDER THESE *GIANT IRON ORE DEPOSITS!*

SO YOU WANT US TO DIG THEM OUT WITH OUR METALBENDING?

THAT'S THE PLAN!

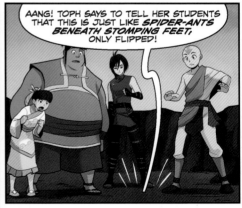

AANG! TOPH SAYS TO TELL HER STUDENTS THAT THIS IS JUST LIKE *SPIDER-ANTS BENEATH STOMPING FEET,* ONLY FLIPPED!

THAT MEAN SOMETHING TO YOU GUYS?

SPIDER-ANTS BENEATH STOMPING FEET?! MY SOUL IS ABLAZE WITH EBON ANXIOUSNESS!

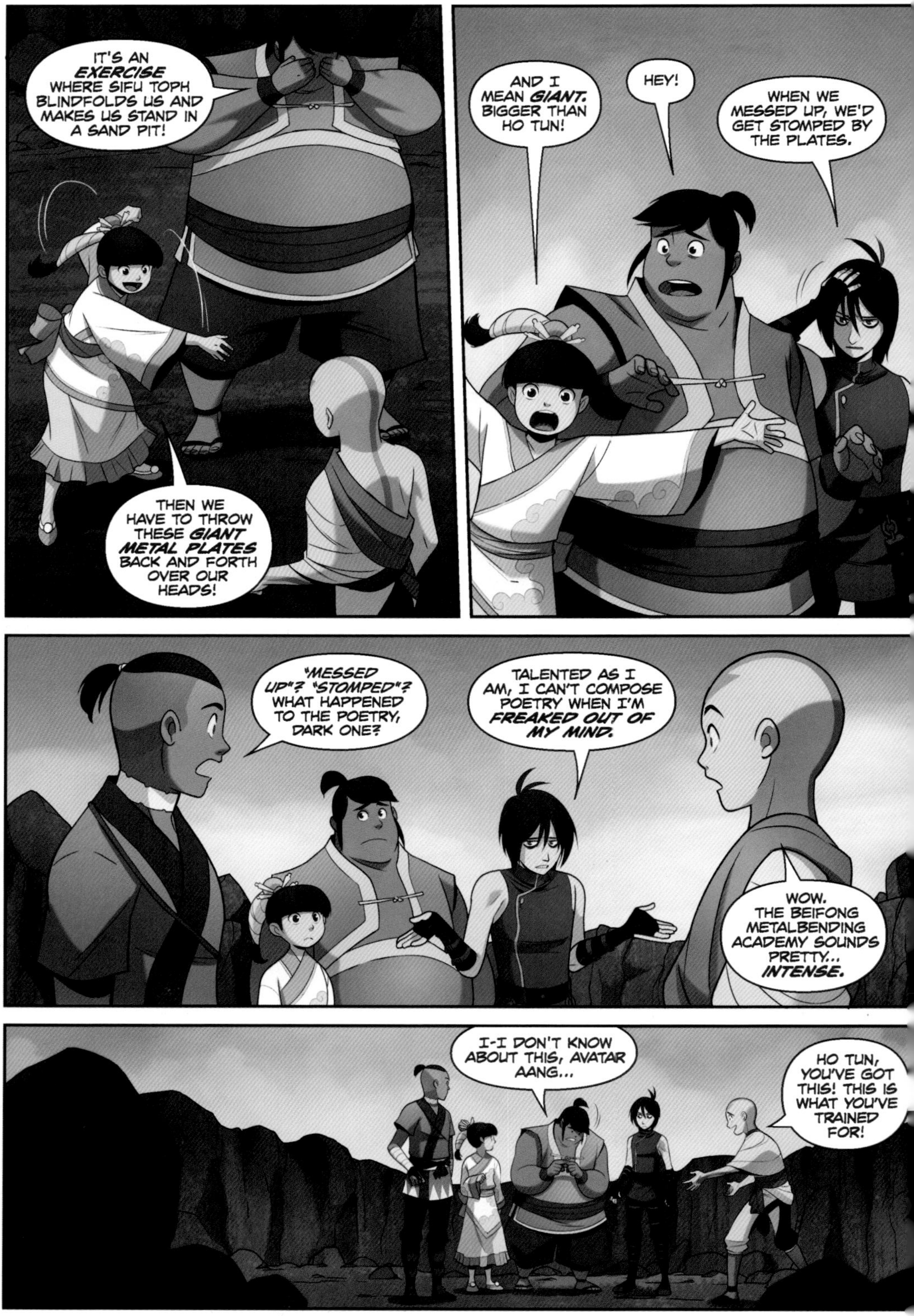
IT'S AN EXERCISE WHERE SIFU TOPH BLINDFOLDS US AND MAKES US STAND IN A SAND PIT!
THEN WE HAVE TO THROW THESE GIANT METAL PLATES BACK AND FORTH OVER OUR HEADS!
AND I MEAN GIANT. BIGGER THAN HO TUN!
HEY!
WHEN WE MESSED UP, WE'D GET STOMPED BY THE PLATES.
"MESSED UP"? "STOMPED"? WHAT HAPPENED TO THE POETRY, DARK ONE?
TALENTED AS I AM, I CAN'T COMPOSE POETRY WHEN I'M FREAKED OUT OF MY MIND.
WOW. THE BEIFONG METALBENDING ACADEMY SOUNDS PRETTY... INTENSE.
I-I DON'T KNOW ABOUT THIS, AVATAR AANG...
HO TUN, YOU'VE GOT THIS! THIS IS WHAT YOU'VE TRAINED FOR!

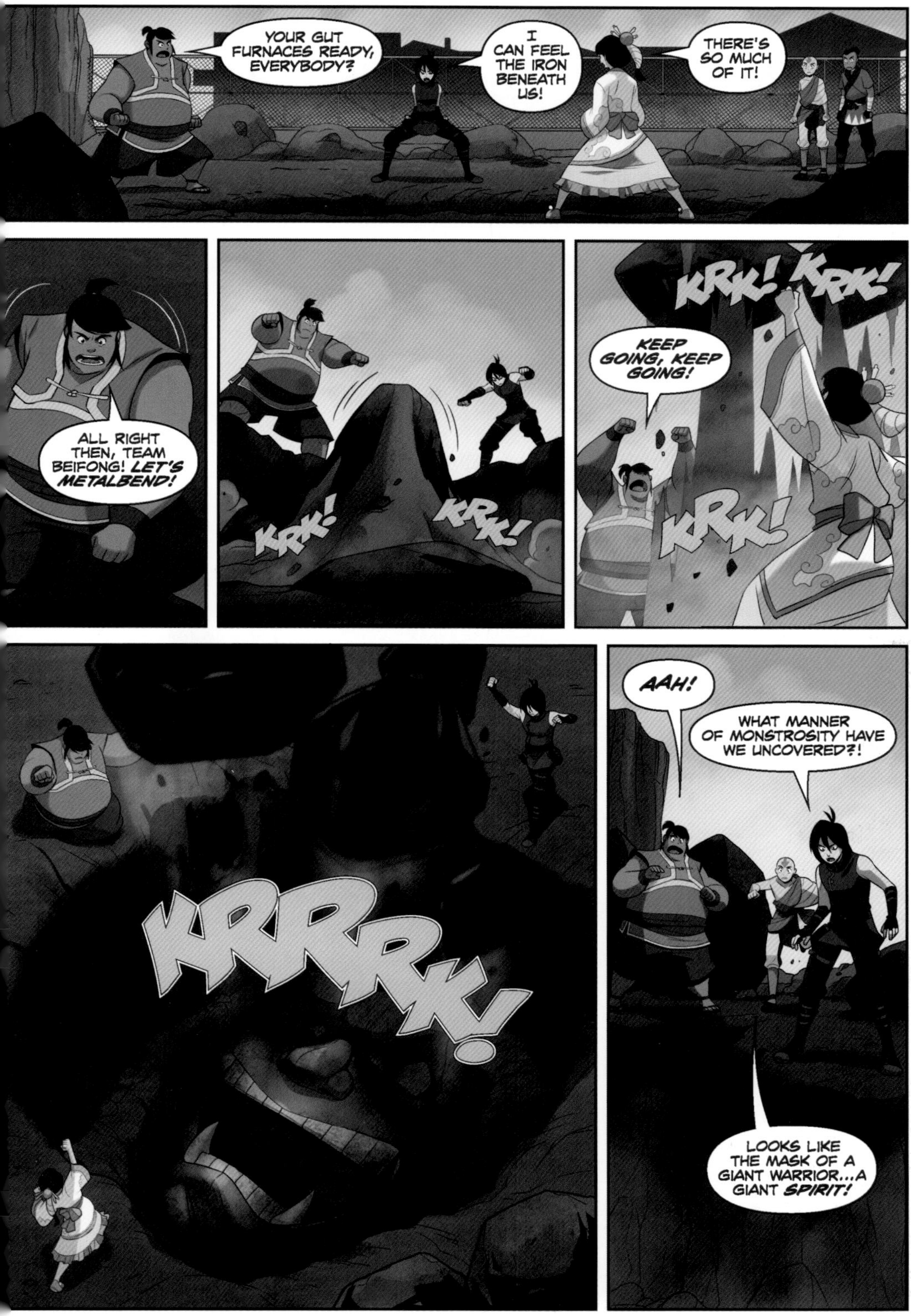
YOUR GUT FURNACES READY, EVERYBODY?
I CAN FEEL THE IRON BENEATH US!
THERE'S SO MUCH OF IT!
ALL RIGHT THEN, TEAM BEIFONG! LET'S METALBEND!
KRK!
KRK!
KRK! KRK!
KEEP GOING, KEEP GOING!
KRK!
KRRRRK!
AAH!
WHAT MANNER OF MONSTROSITY HAVE WE UNCOVERED?!
LOOKS LIKE THE MASK OF A GIANT WARRIOR...A GIANT SPIRIT!

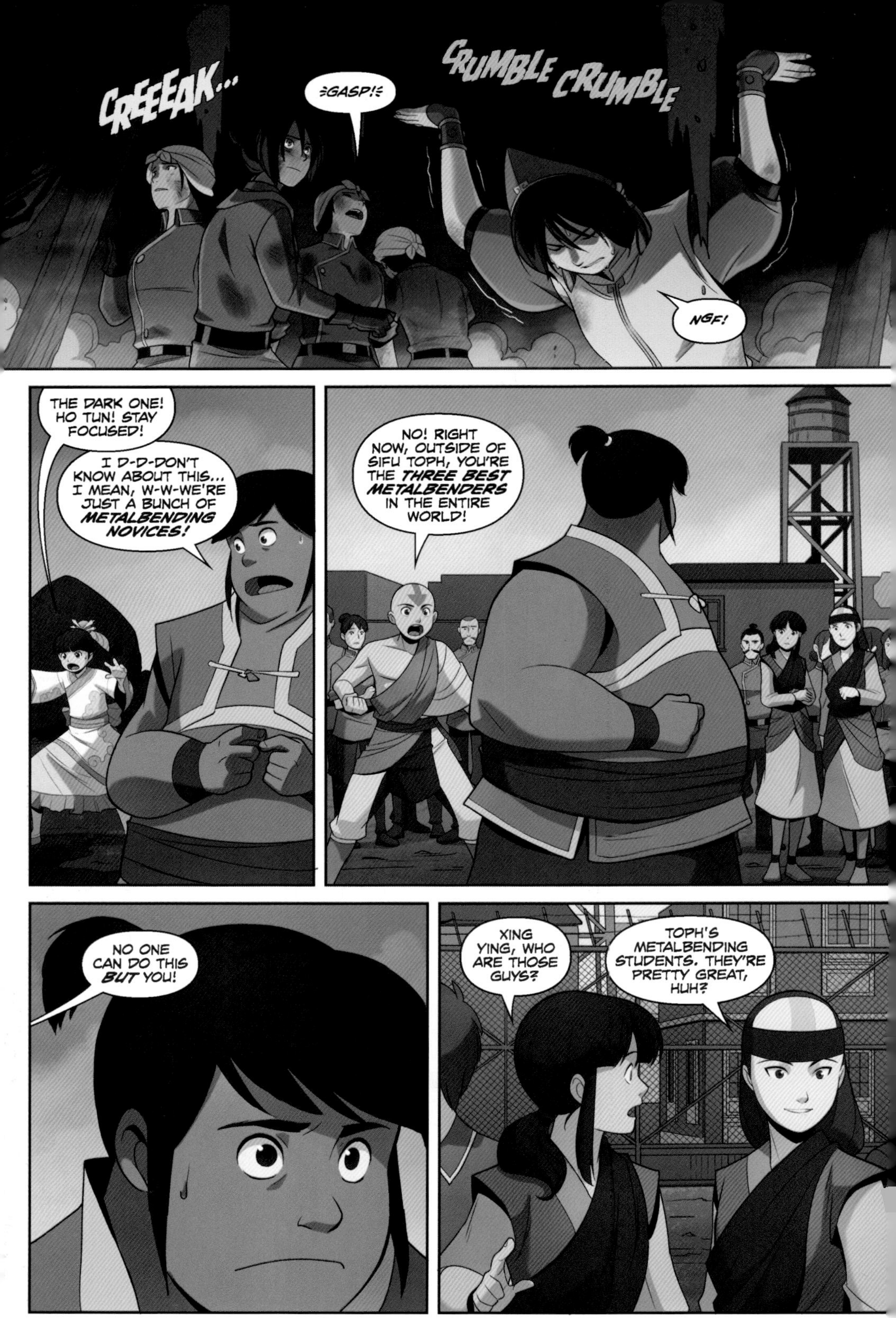
CREEEAK...
GASP!
CRUMBLE CRUMBLE
NGF!
THE DARK ONE! HO TUN! STAY FOCUSED!
I D-D-DON'T KNOW ABOUT THIS... I MEAN, W-W-WE'RE JUST A BUNCH OF METALBENDING NOVICES!
NO! RIGHT NOW, OUTSIDE OF SIFU TOPH, YOU'RE THE THREE BEST METALBENDERS IN THE ENTIRE WORLD!
NO ONE CAN DO THIS BUT YOU!
XING YING, WHO ARE THOSE GUYS?
TOPH'S METALBENDING STUDENTS. THEY'RE PRETTY GREAT, HUH?

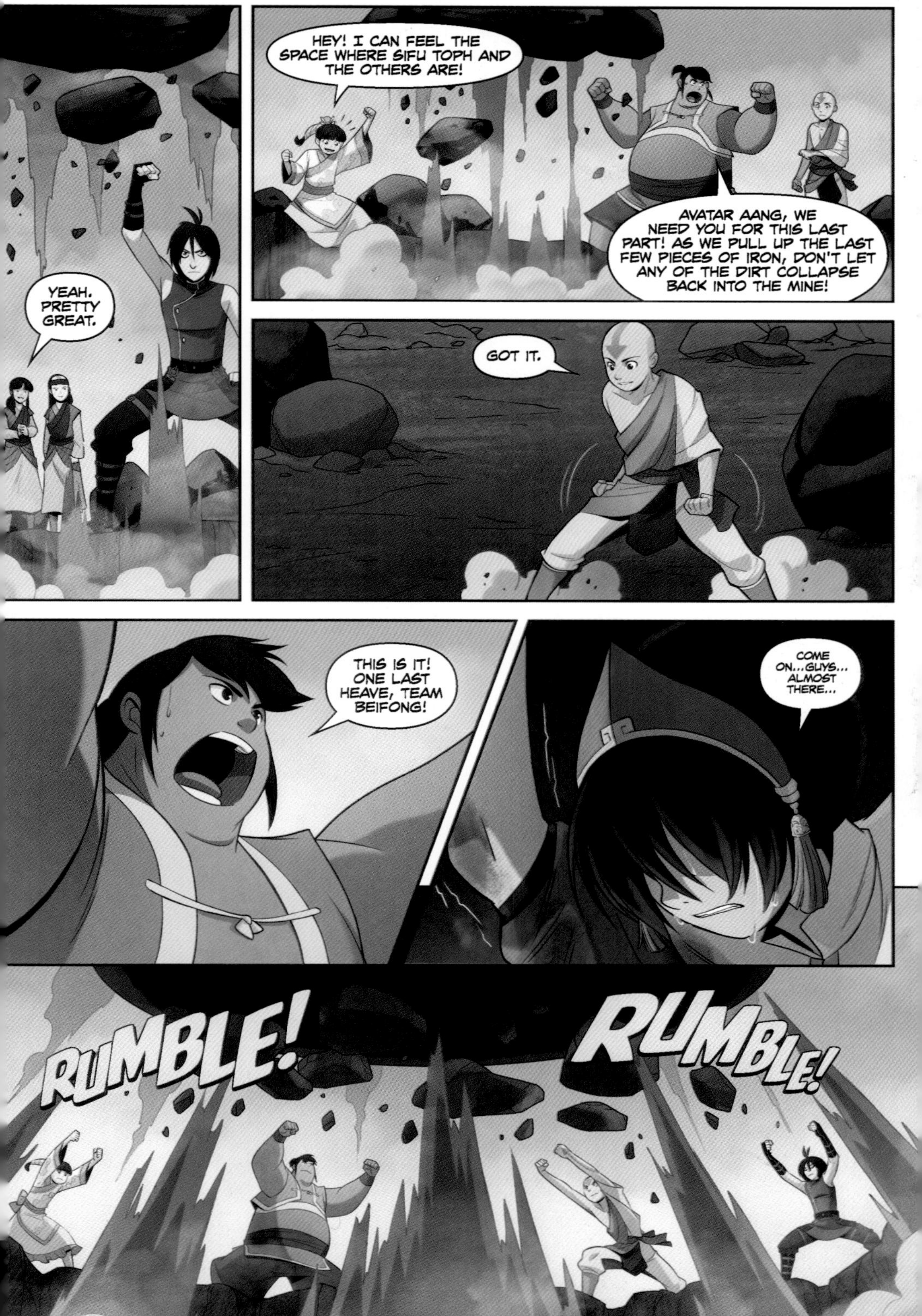
HEY! I CAN FEEL THE SPACE WHERE SIFU TOPH AND THE OTHERS ARE!
AVATAR AANG, WE NEED YOU FOR THIS LAST PART! AS WE PULL UP THE LAST FEW PIECES OF IRON, DON'T LET ANY OF THE DIRT COLLAPSE BACK INTO THE MINE!
YEAH. PRETTY GREAT.
GOT IT.
THIS IS IT! ONE LAST HEAVE, TEAM BEIFONG!
COME ON...GUYS... ALMOST THERE...
RUMBLE!
RUMBLE!

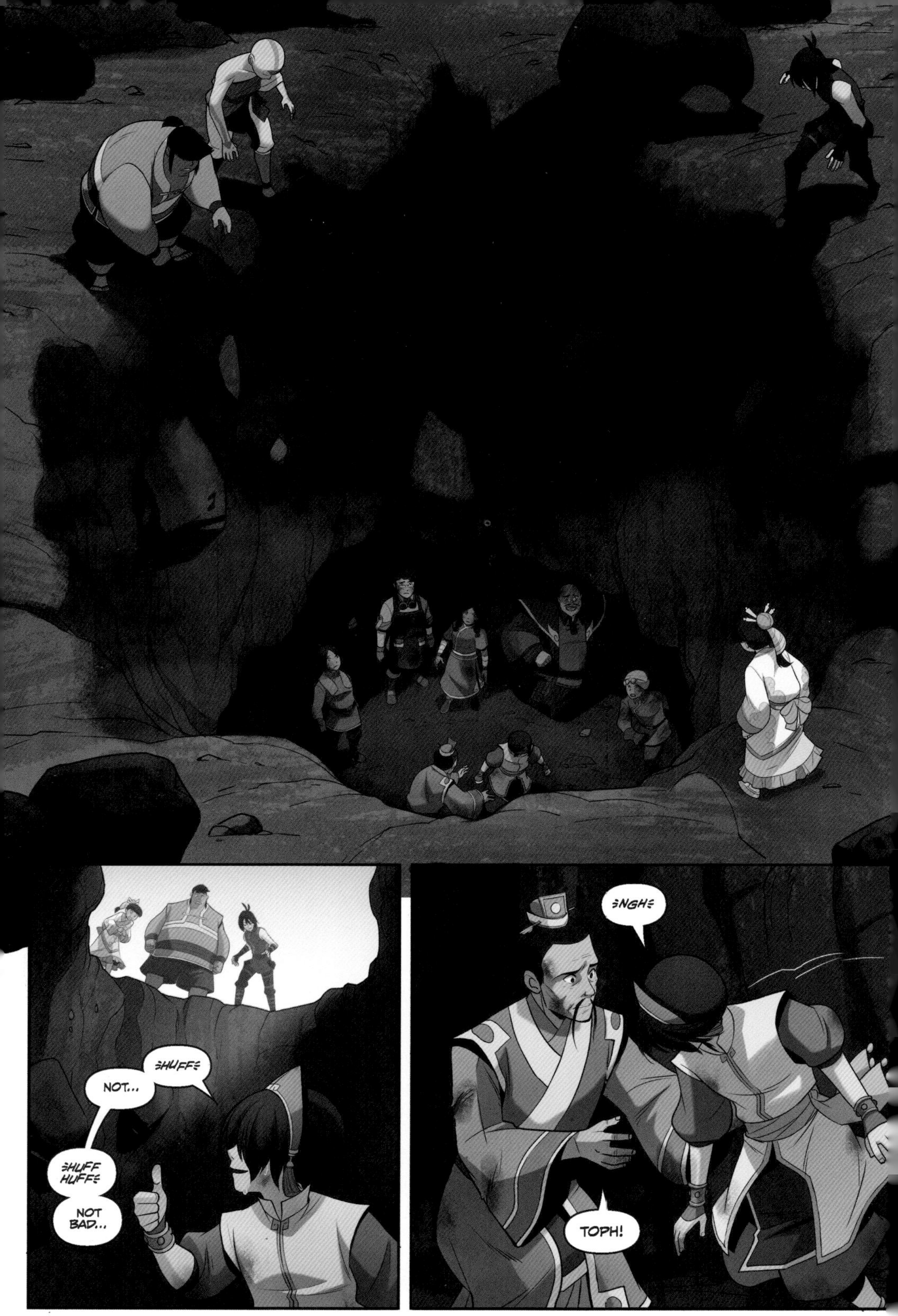

NOT...
HUFF
HUFF HUFF
NOT BAD...
NGH
TOPH!

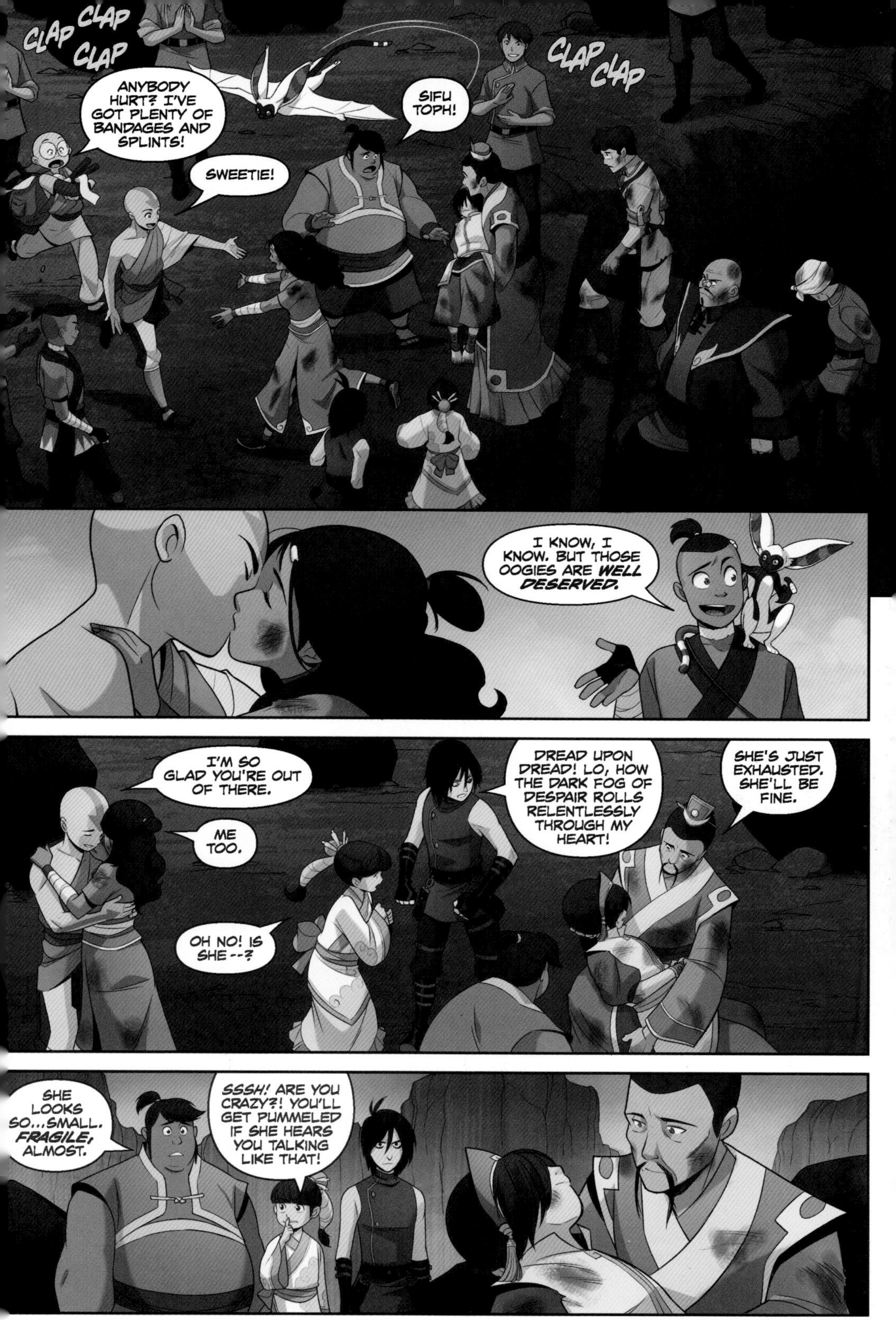
CLAP CLAP CLAP
ANYBODY HURT? I'VE GOT PLENTY OF BANDAGES AND SPLINTS!
SWEETIE!
SIFU TOPH!
CLAP CLAP
I KNOW, I KNOW. BUT THOSE OOGIES ARE WELL DESERVED.
I'M SO GLAD YOU'RE OUT OF THERE.
ME TOO.
OH NO! IS SHE--?
DREAD UPON DREAD! LO, HOW THE DARK FOG OF DESPAIR ROLLS RELENTLESSLY THROUGH MY HEART!
SHE'S JUST EXHAUSTED. SHE'LL BE FINE.
SHE LOOKS SO...SMALL. FRAGILE, ALMOST.
SSSH! ARE YOU CRAZY?! YOU'LL GET PUMMELED IF SHE HEARS YOU TALKING LIKE THAT!

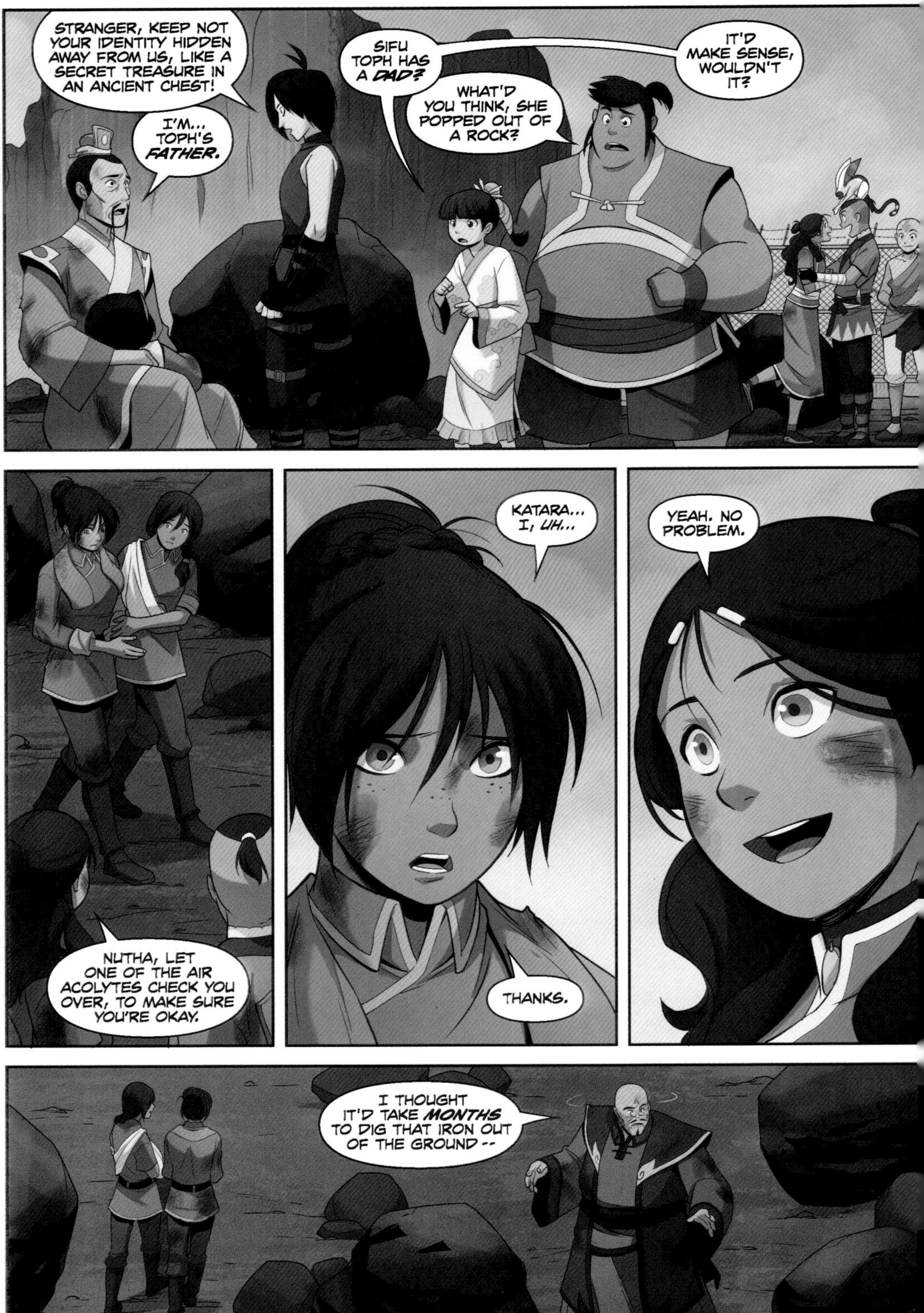
STRANGER, KEEP NOT YOUR IDENTITY HIDDEN AWAY FROM US, LIKE A SECRET TREASURE IN AN ANCIENT CHEST!
I'M... TOPH'S FATHER.
SIFU TOPH HAS A DAD?
WHAT'D YOU THINK, SHE POPPED OUT OF A ROCK?
IT'D MAKE SENSE, WOULDN'T IT?
NUTHA, LET ONE OF THE AIR ACOLYTES CHECK YOU OVER, TO MAKE SURE YOU'RE OKAY.
KATARA... I, UH...
THANKS.
YEAH. NO PROBLEM.
I THOUGHT IT'D TAKE MONTHS TO DIG THAT IRON OUT OF THE GROUND --

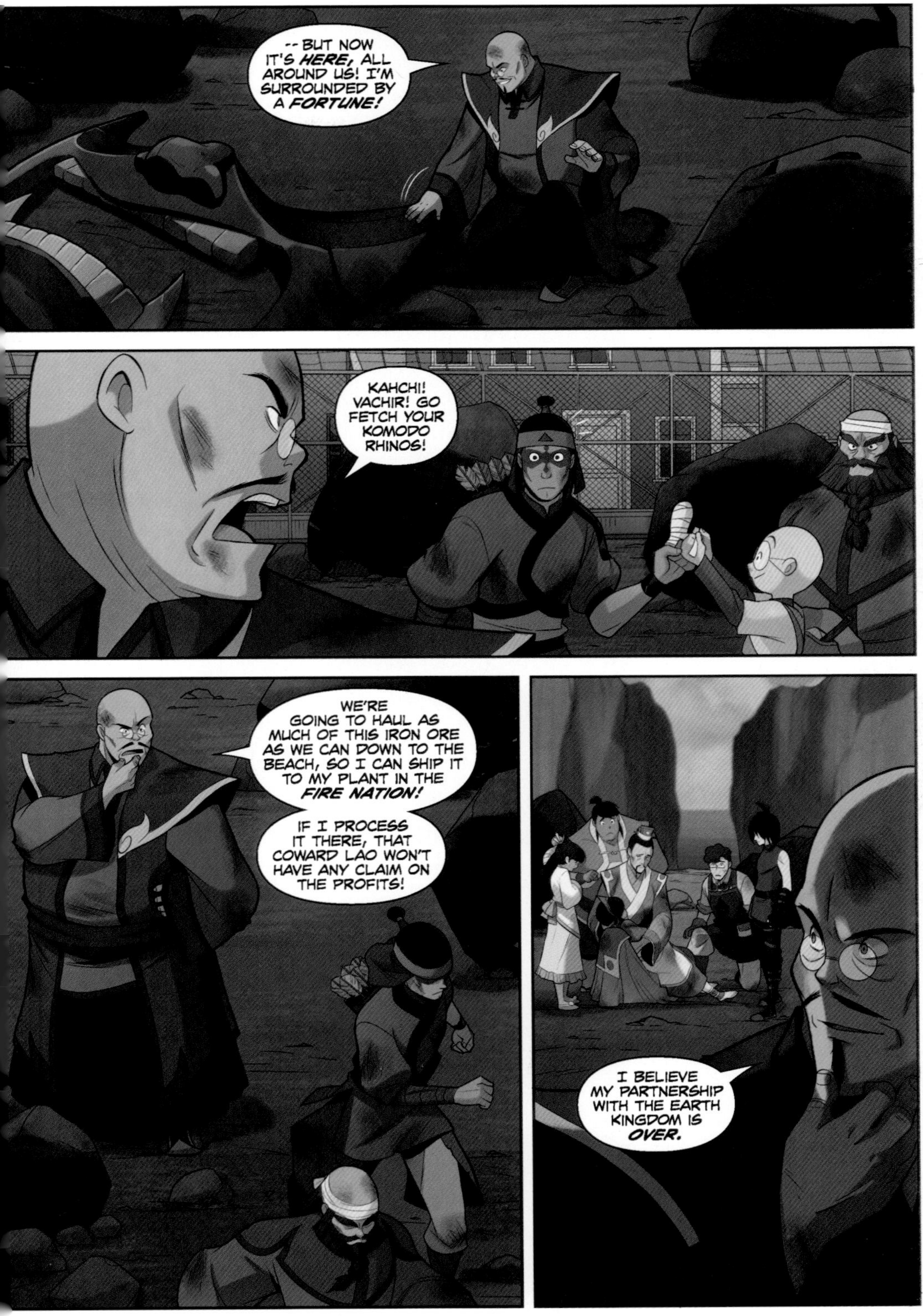
-- BUT NOW IT'S HERE, ALL AROUND US! I'M SURROUNDED BY A FORTUNE!
KAHCHI! VACHIR! GO FETCH YOUR KOMODO RHINOS!
WE'RE GOING TO HAUL AS MUCH OF THIS IRON ORE AS WE CAN DOWN TO THE BEACH, SO I CAN SHIP IT TO MY PLANT IN THE FIRE NATION!
IF I PROCESS IT THERE, THAT COWARD LAO WON'T HAVE ANY CLAIM ON THE PROFITS!
I BELIEVE MY PARTNERSHIP WITH THE EARTH KINGDOM IS OVER.

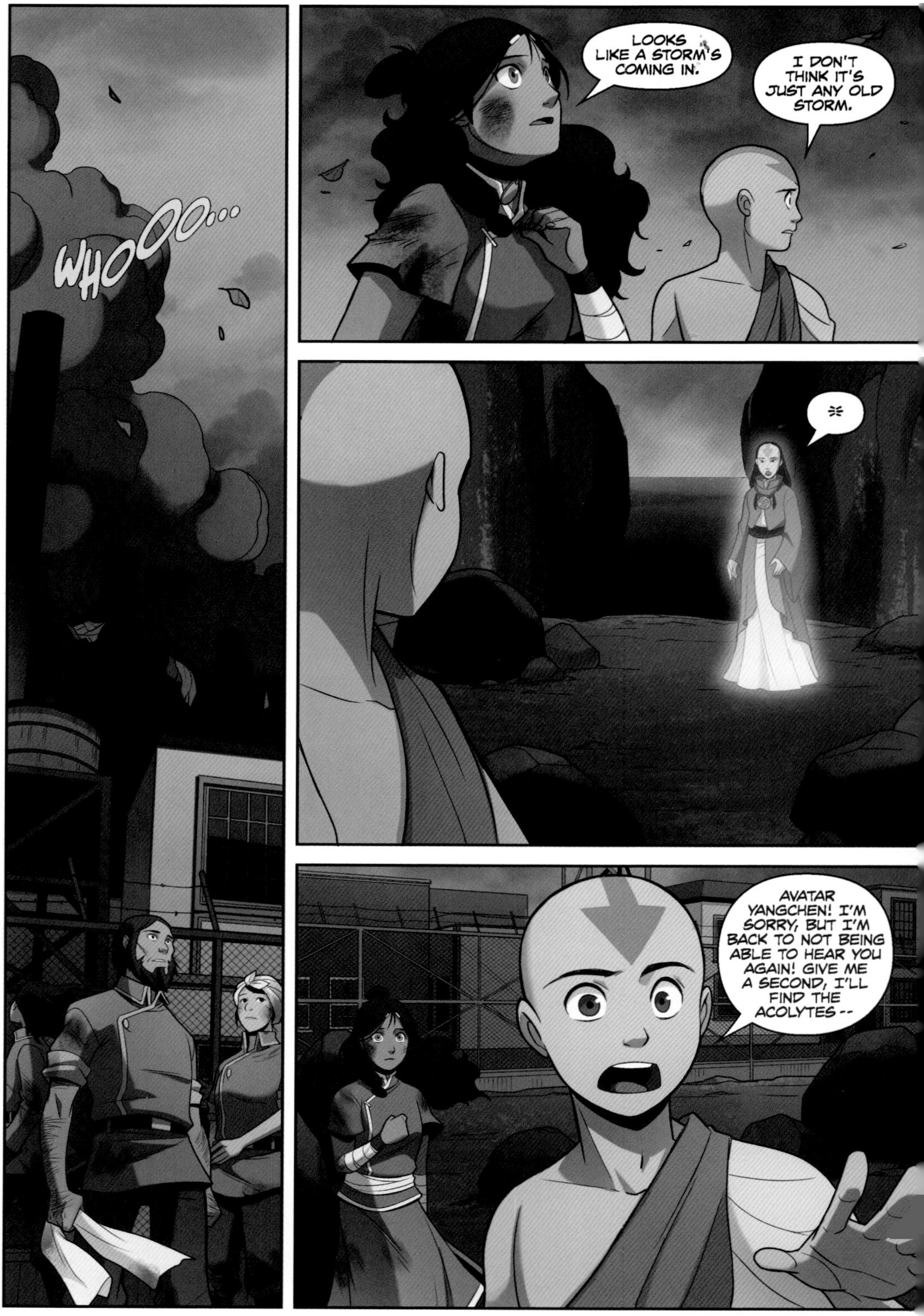
WHOOOO...
LOOKS LIKE A STORM'S COMING IN.
I DON'T THINK IT'S JUST ANY OLD STORM.
AVATAR YANGCHEN! I'M SORRY, BUT I'M BACK TO NOT BEING ABLE TO HEAR YOU AGAIN! GIVE ME A SECOND, I'LL FIND THE ACOLYTES --

GUYS, I NEED TO FINISH THE *CEREMONIAL MEAL!* YOU STILL HAVE THE FOOD AND THE INCENSE AND THE OTHER STUFF?

KIND OF...

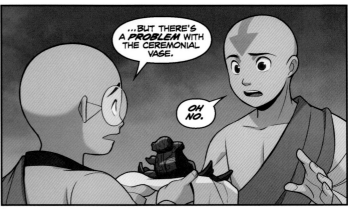

...BUT THERE'S A *PROBLEM* WITH THE CEREMONIAL VASE.

OH NO.

THERE'S GOTTA BE ANOTHER WAY...

LIKE YOUR MEDITATION BEADS, THE AVATARS ARE LINKED, ONE TO THE OTHER.

ANYTHING I CAN DO TO HELP?

NO, I GOT THIS. I JUST NEED SOME PEACE, QUIET, AND A *GOOD-SIZED ROCK.*

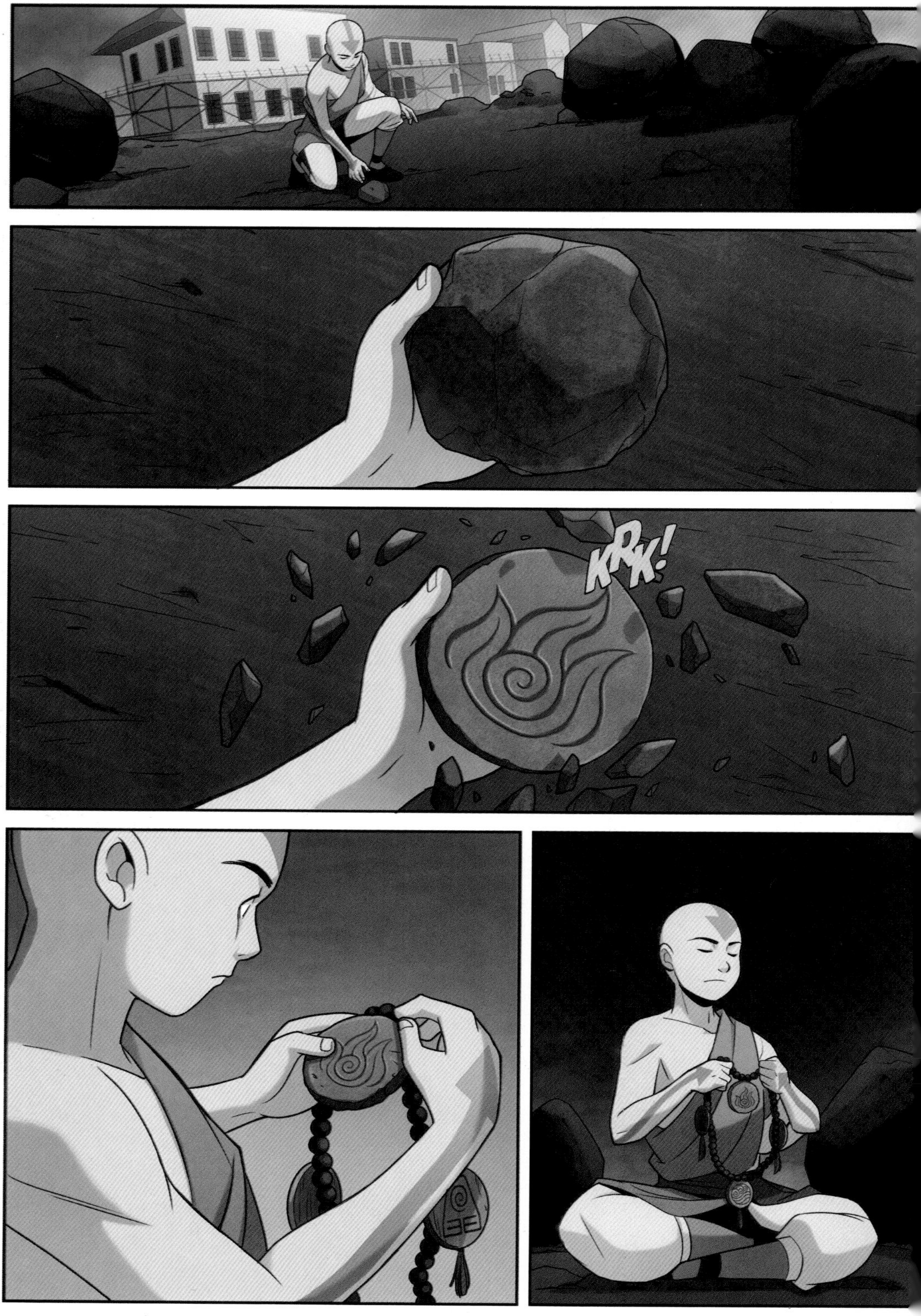
KRK!

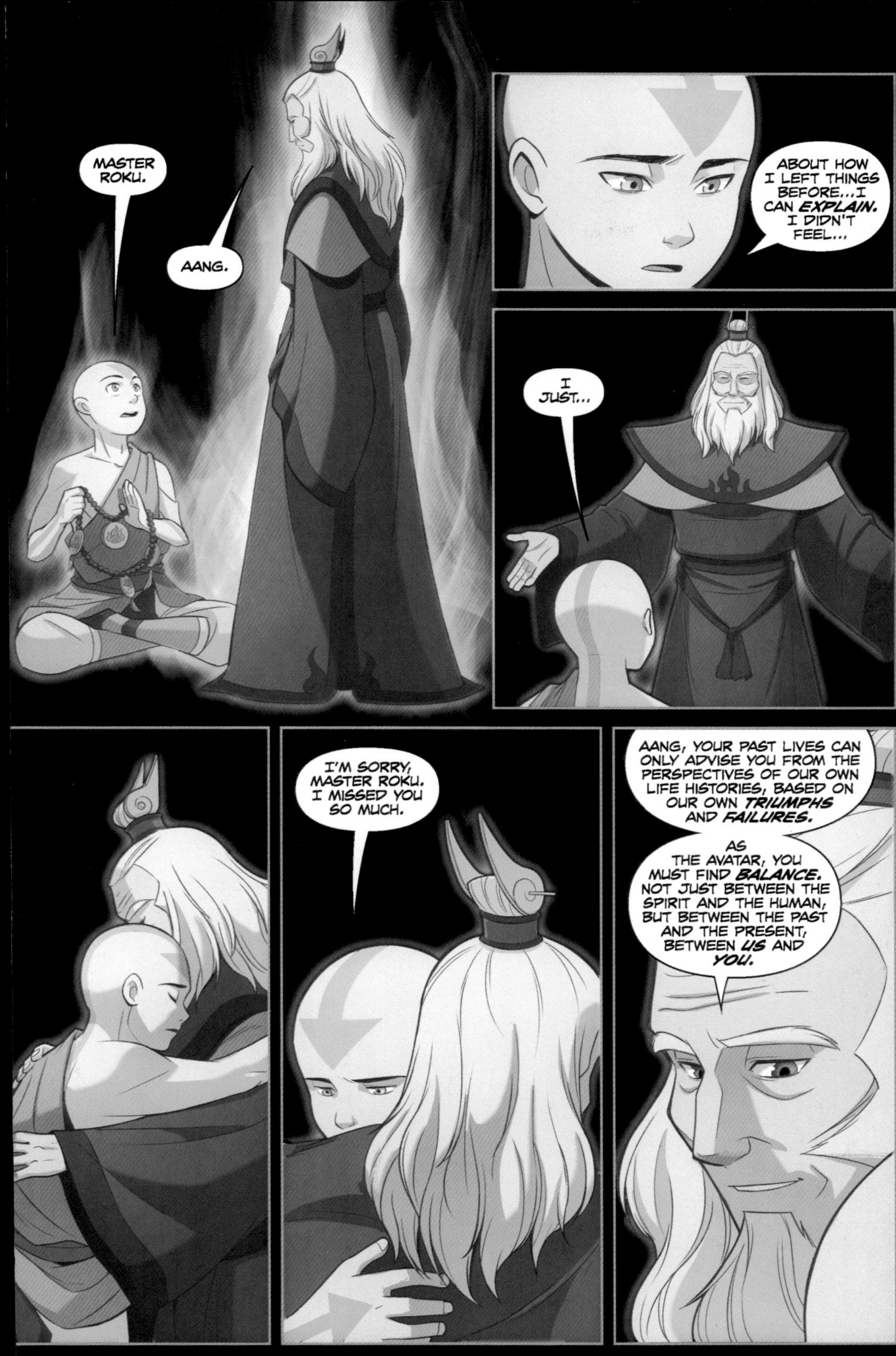
MASTER ROKU.
AANG.
ABOUT HOW I LEFT THINGS BEFORE...I CAN *EXPLAIN.* I DIDN'T FEEL...
I JUST...
I'M SORRY, MASTER ROKU. I MISSED YOU SO MUCH.
AANG, YOUR PAST LIVES CAN ONLY ADVISE YOU FROM THE PERSPECTIVES OF OUR OWN LIFE HISTORIES, BASED ON OUR OWN *TRIUMPHS* AND *FAILURES.*
AS THE AVATAR, YOU MUST FIND *BALANCE.* NOT JUST BETWEEN THE SPIRIT AND THE HUMAN, BUT BETWEEN THE PAST AND THE PRESENT, BETWEEN *US* AND *YOU.*

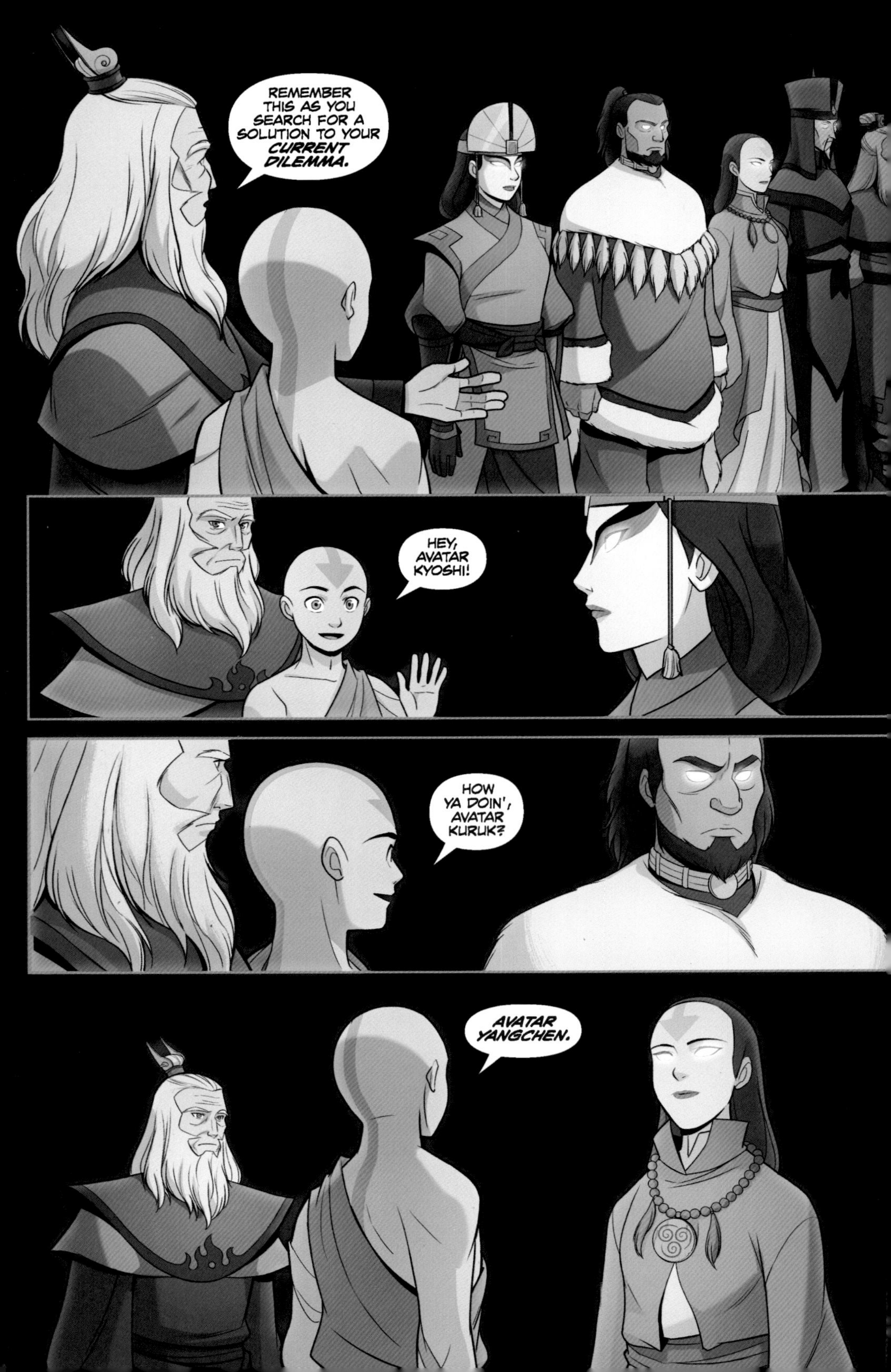
REMEMBER THIS AS YOU SEARCH FOR A SOLUTION TO YOUR *CURRENT DILEMMA.*
HEY, AVATAR KYOSHI!
HOW YA DOIN', AVATAR KURUK?
AVATAR YANGCHEN.

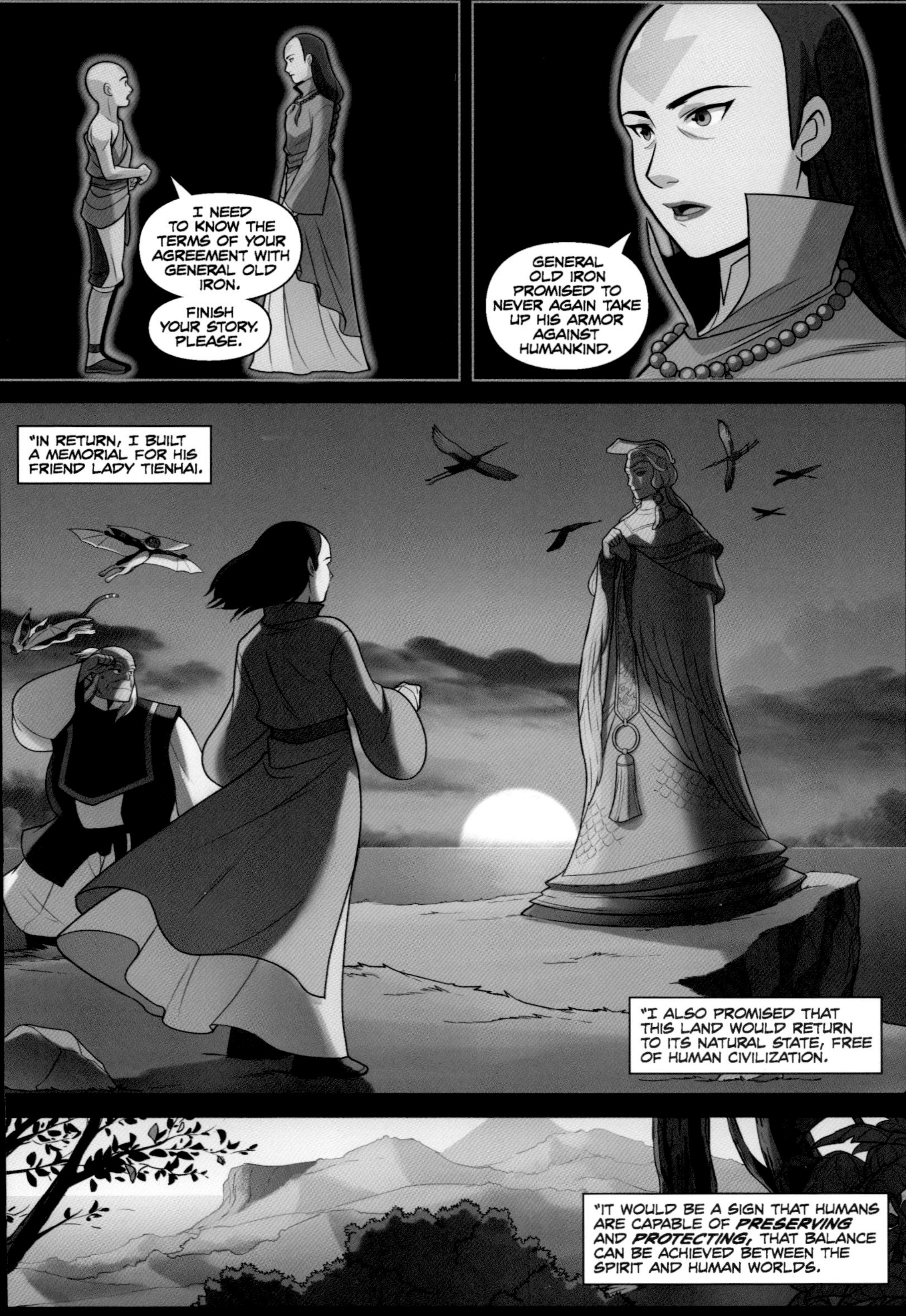
I NEED TO KNOW THE TERMS OF YOUR AGREEMENT WITH GENERAL OLD IRON.
FINISH YOUR STORY. PLEASE.
GENERAL OLD IRON PROMISED TO NEVER AGAIN TAKE UP HIS ARMOR AGAINST HUMANKIND.
"IN RETURN, I BUILT A MEMORIAL FOR HIS FRIEND LADY TIENHAI.
"I ALSO PROMISED THAT THIS LAND WOULD RETURN TO ITS NATURAL STATE, FREE OF HUMAN CIVILIZATION.
"IT WOULD BE A SIGN THAT HUMANS ARE CAPABLE OF ***PRESERVING*** AND ***PROTECTING,*** THAT BALANCE CAN BE ACHIEVED BETWEEN THE SPIRIT AND HUMAN WORLDS.

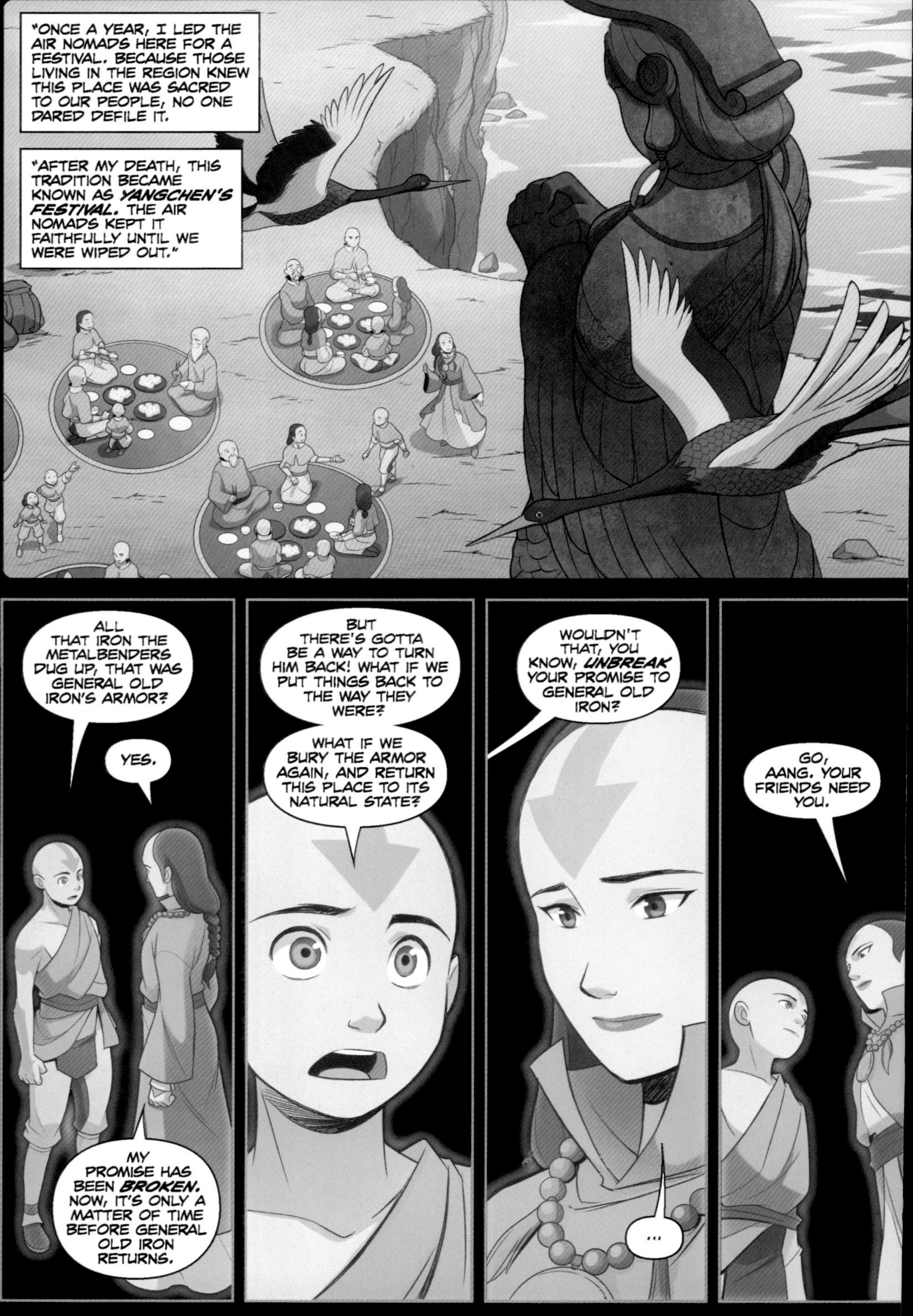
"ONCE A YEAR, I LED THE AIR NOMADS HERE FOR A FESTIVAL. BECAUSE THOSE LIVING IN THE REGION KNEW THIS PLACE WAS SACRED TO OUR PEOPLE, NO ONE DARED DEFILE IT.
"AFTER MY DEATH, THIS TRADITION BECAME KNOWN AS *YANGCHEN'S FESTIVAL.* THE AIR NOMADS KEPT IT FAITHFULLY UNTIL WE WERE WIPED OUT."
ALL THAT IRON THE METALBENDERS DUG UP, THAT WAS GENERAL OLD IRON'S ARMOR?
YES.
MY PROMISE HAS BEEN *BROKEN.* NOW, IT'S ONLY A MATTER OF TIME BEFORE GENERAL OLD IRON RETURNS.
BUT THERE'S GOTTA BE A WAY TO TURN HIM BACK! WHAT IF WE PUT THINGS BACK TO THE WAY THEY WERE?
WHAT IF WE BURY THE ARMOR AGAIN, AND RETURN THIS PLACE TO ITS NATURAL STATE?
WOULDN'T THAT, YOU KNOW, *UNBREAK* YOUR PROMISE TO GENERAL OLD IRON?
...
GO, AANG. YOUR FRIENDS NEED YOU.

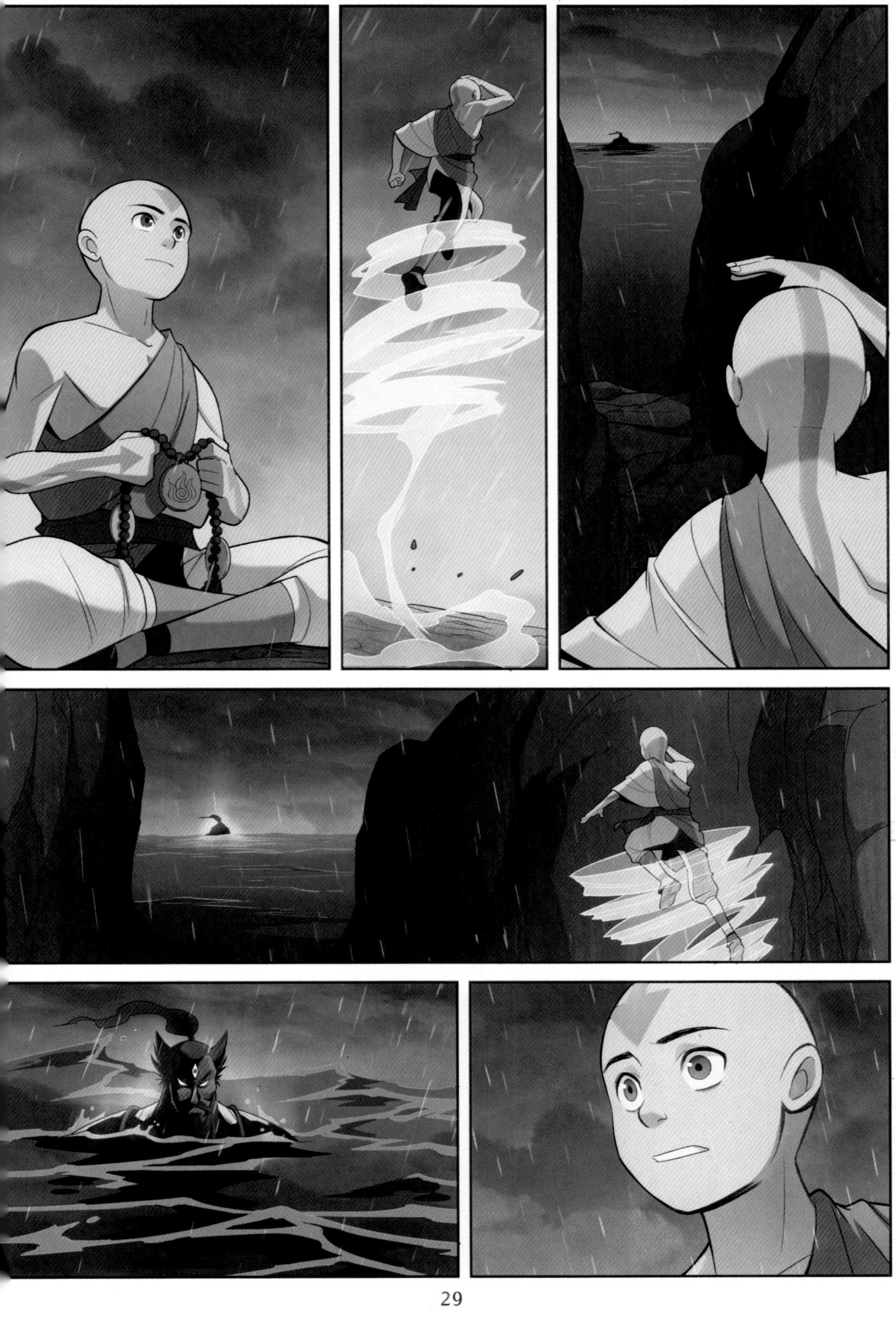

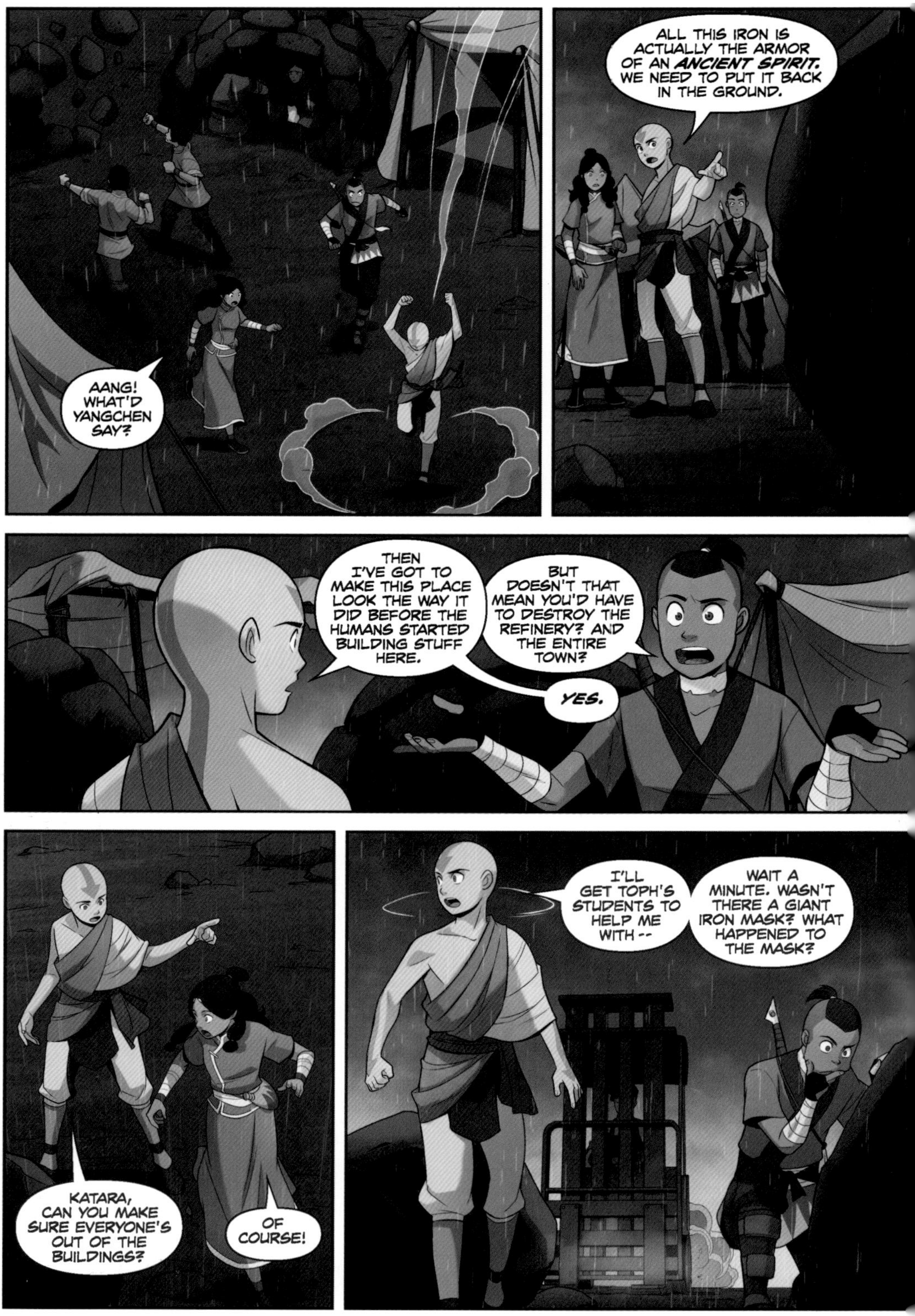
AANG! WHAT'D YANGCHEN SAY?
ALL THIS IRON IS ACTUALLY THE ARMOR OF AN ***ANCIENT SPIRIT.*** WE NEED TO PUT IT BACK IN THE GROUND.
THEN I'VE GOT TO MAKE THIS PLACE LOOK THE WAY IT DID BEFORE THE HUMANS STARTED BUILDING STUFF HERE.
BUT DOESN'T THAT MEAN YOU'D HAVE TO DESTROY THE REFINERY? AND THE ENTIRE TOWN?
YES.
KATARA, CAN YOU MAKE SURE EVERYONE'S OUT OF THE BUILDINGS?
OF COURSE!
I'LL GET TOPH'S STUDENTS TO HELP ME WITH --
WAIT A MINUTE. WASN'T THERE A GIANT IRON MASK? WHAT HAPPENED TO THE MASK?

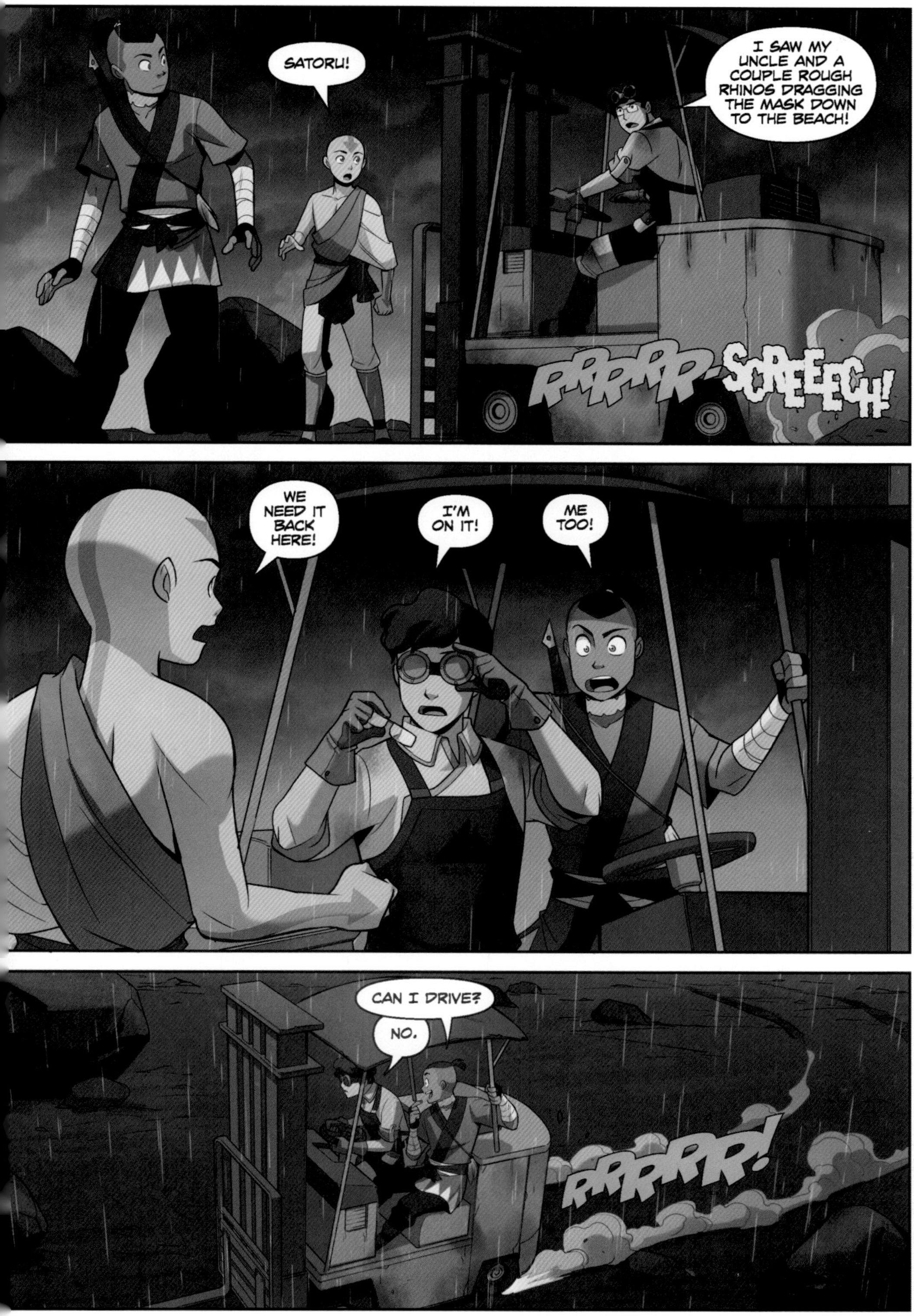
SATORU!
I SAW MY UNCLE AND A COUPLE ROUGH RHINOS DRAGGING THE MASK DOWN TO THE BEACH!
RRRRR-SCREEECH!
WE NEED IT BACK HERE!
I'M ON IT!
ME TOO!
CAN I DRIVE?
NO.
RRRRR!

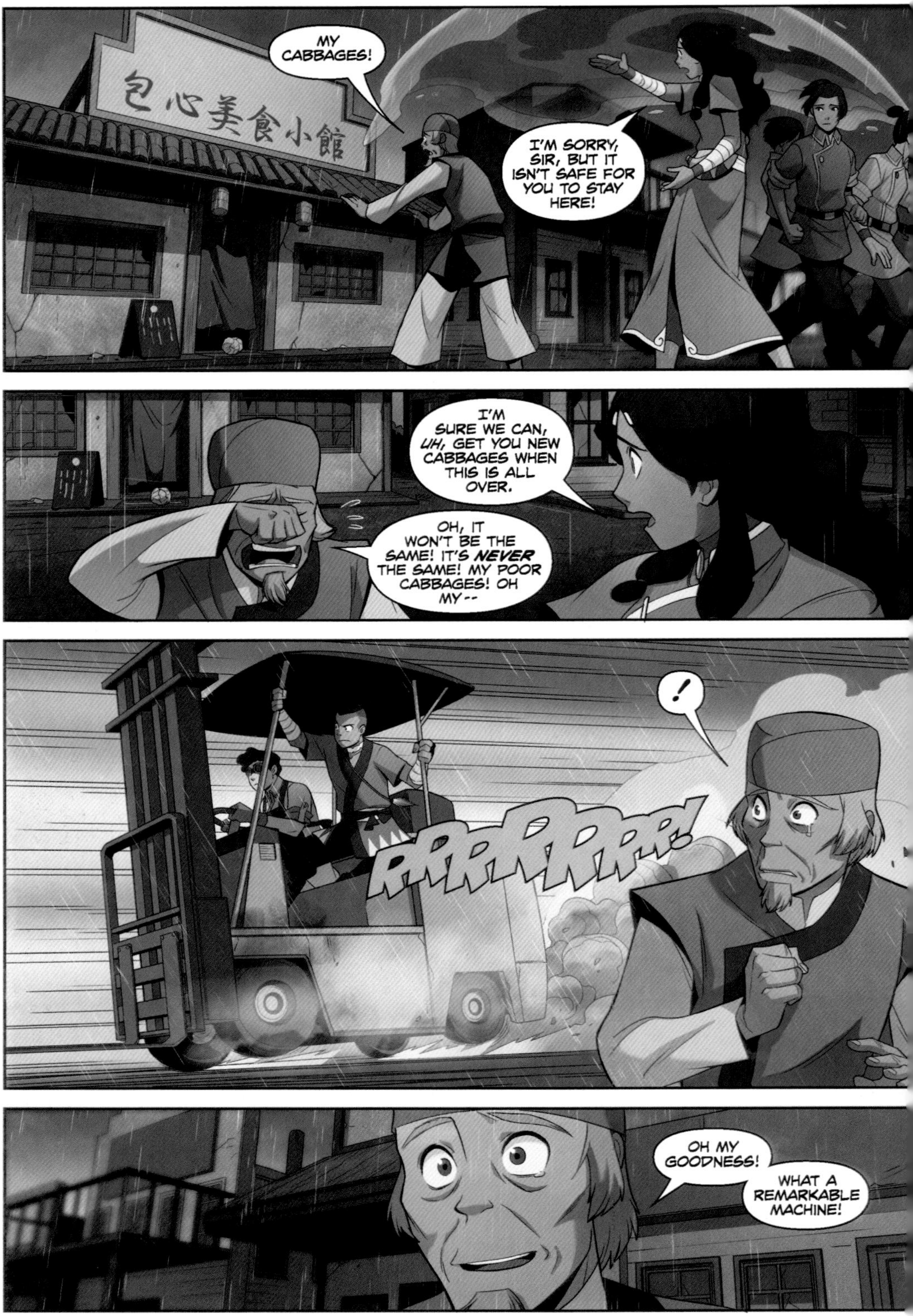
包心美食小館
MY CABBAGES!
I'M SORRY, SIR, BUT IT ISN'T SAFE FOR YOU TO STAY HERE!
I'M SURE WE CAN, *UH,* GET YOU NEW CABBAGES WHEN THIS IS ALL OVER.
OH, IT WON'T BE THE SAME! IT'S ***NEVER*** THE SAME! MY POOR CABBAGES! OH MY --
RRRRRRRR!
!
OH MY GOODNESS!
WHAT A REMARKABLE MACHINE!

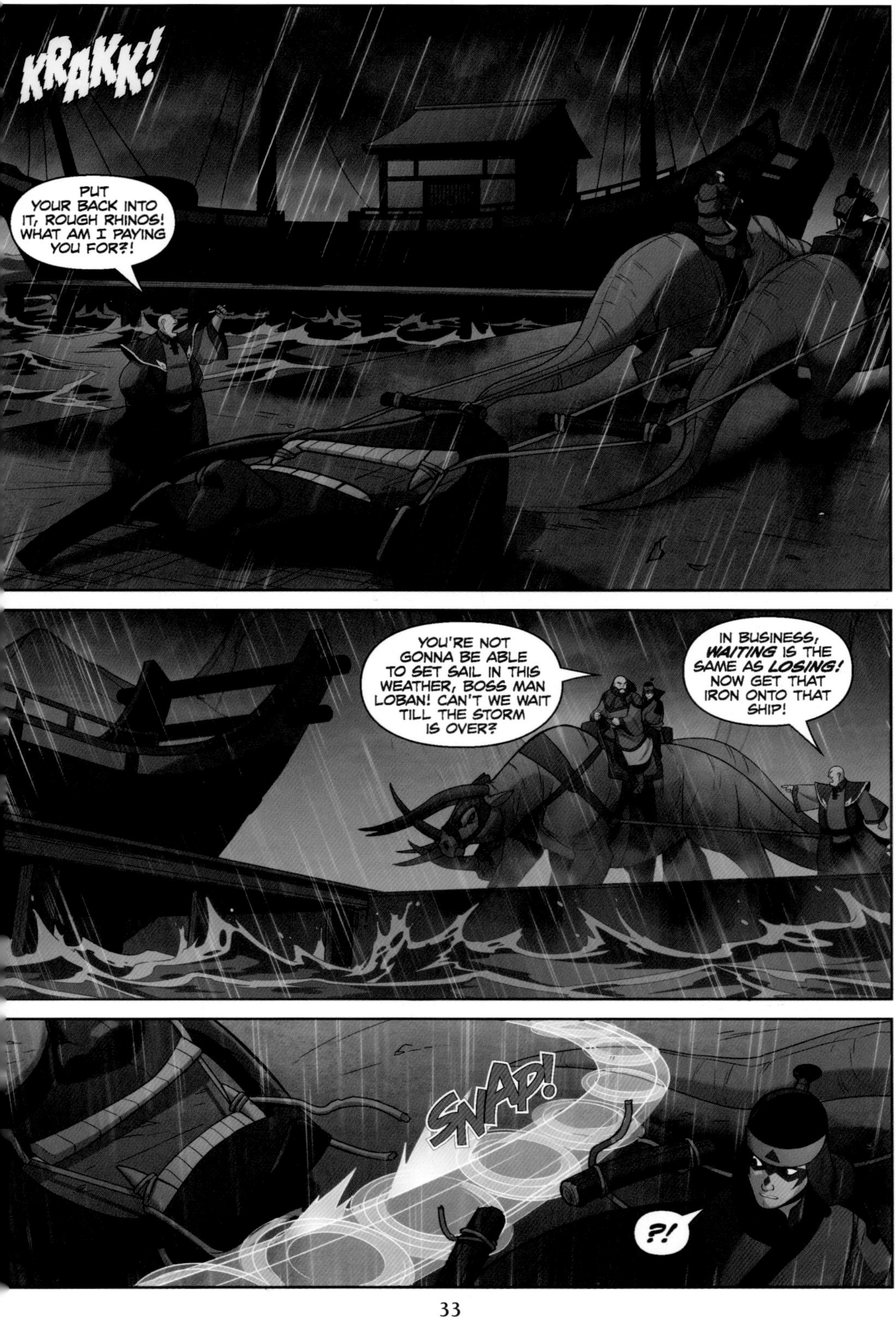
KRAKK!
PUT YOUR BACK INTO IT, ROUGH RHINOS! WHAT AM I PAYING YOU FOR?!
YOU'RE NOT GONNA BE ABLE TO SET SAIL IN THIS WEATHER, BOSS MAN LOBAN! CAN'T WE WAIT TILL THE STORM IS OVER?
IN BUSINESS, WAITING IS THE SAME AS LOSING! NOW GET THAT IRON ONTO THAT SHIP!
SNAP!
?!

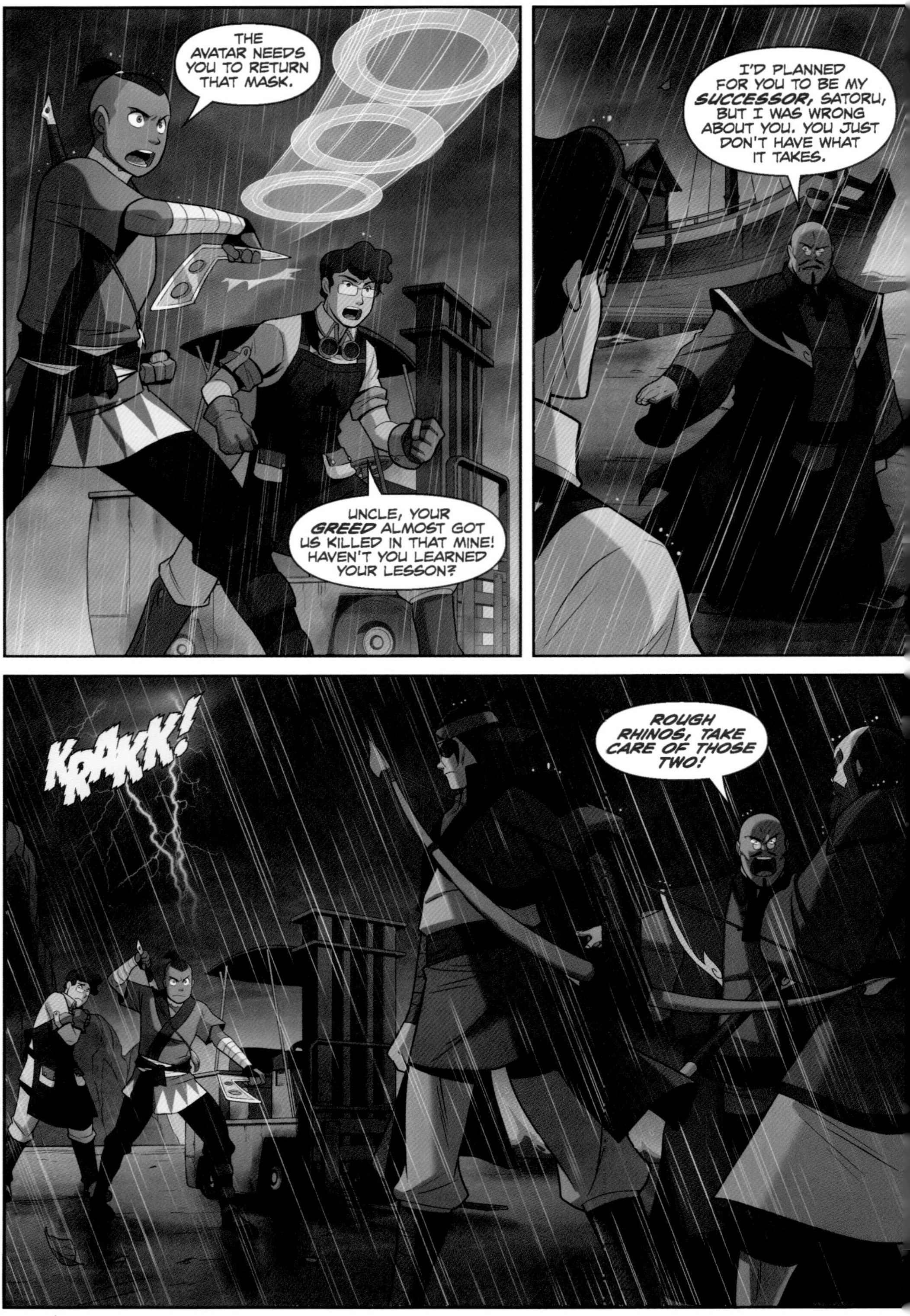
THE AVATAR NEEDS YOU TO RETURN THAT MASK.
UNCLE, YOUR GREED ALMOST GOT US KILLED IN THAT MINE! HAVEN'T YOU LEARNED YOUR LESSON?
I'D PLANNED FOR YOU TO BE MY SUCCESSOR, SATORU, BUT I WAS WRONG ABOUT YOU. YOU JUST DON'T HAVE WHAT IT TAKES.
KRAKK!
ROUGH RHINOS, TAKE CARE OF THOSE TWO!

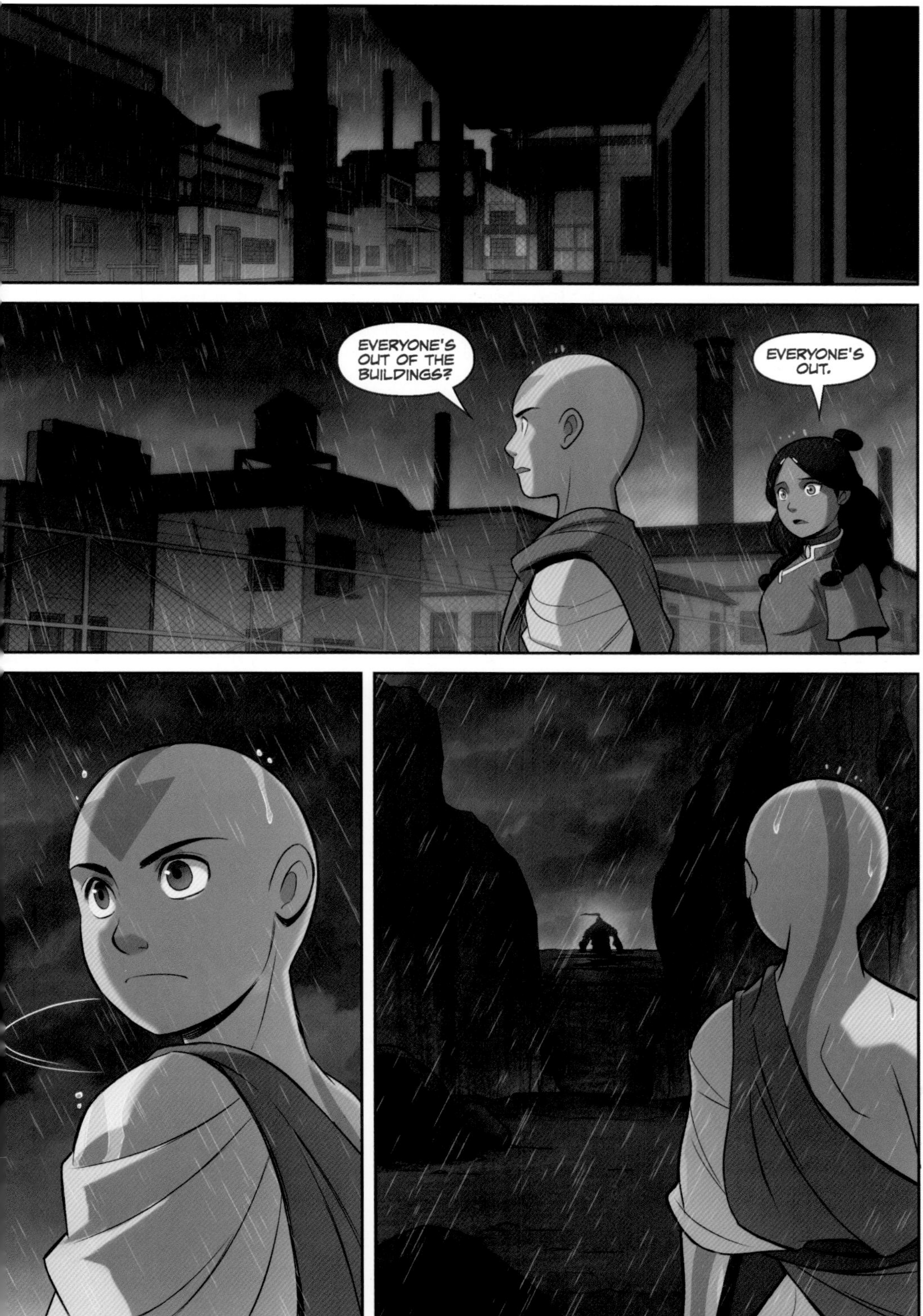
EVERYONE'S OUT OF THE BUILDINGS?
EVERYONE'S OUT.

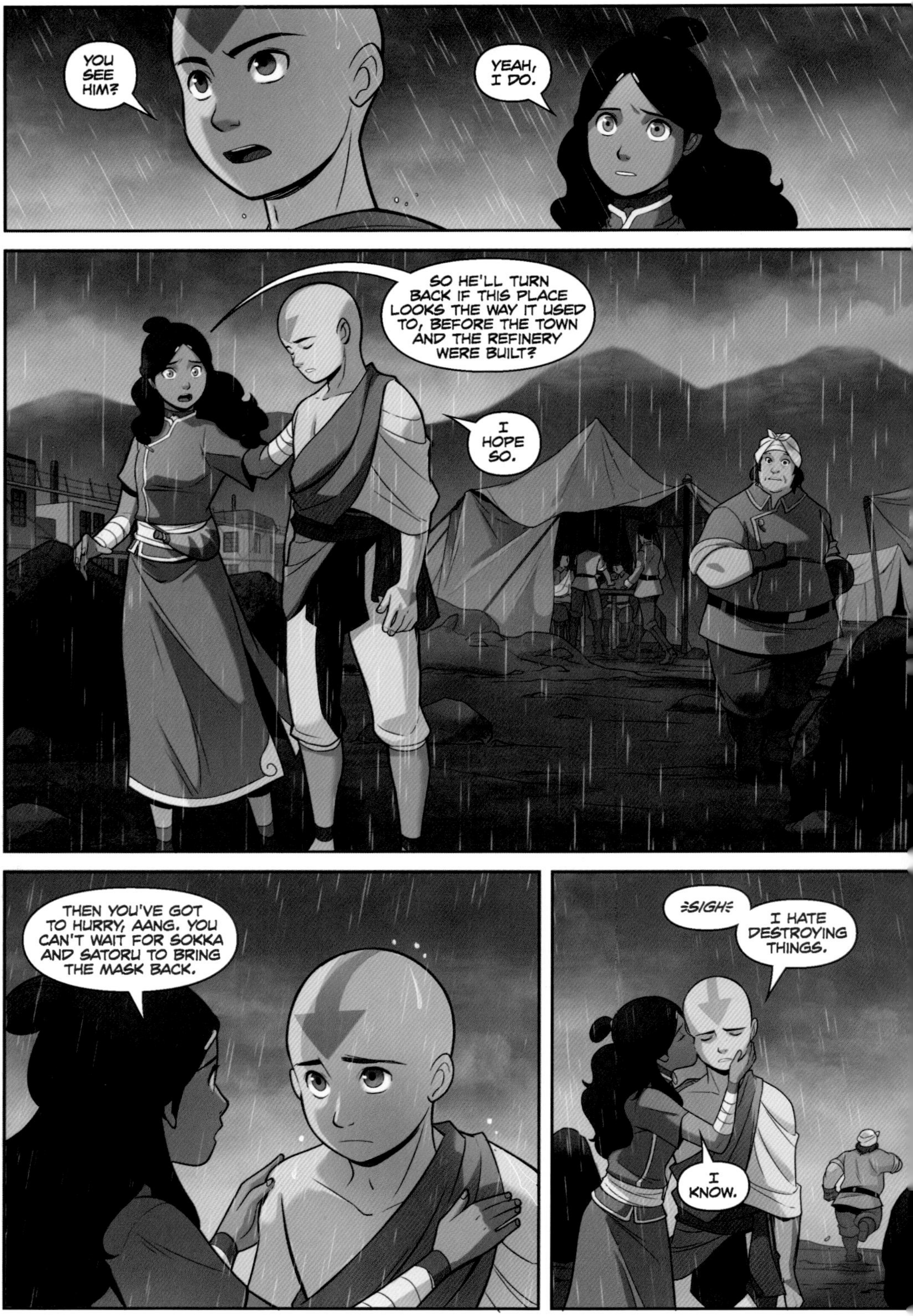
YOU SEE HIM?
YEAH, I DO.
SO HE'LL TURN BACK IF THIS PLACE LOOKS THE WAY IT USED TO, BEFORE THE TOWN AND THE REFINERY WERE BUILT?
I HOPE SO.
THEN YOU'VE GOT TO HURRY, AANG. YOU CAN'T WAIT FOR SOKKA AND SATORU TO BRING THE MASK BACK.
SIGH
I HATE DESTROYING THINGS.
I KNOW.

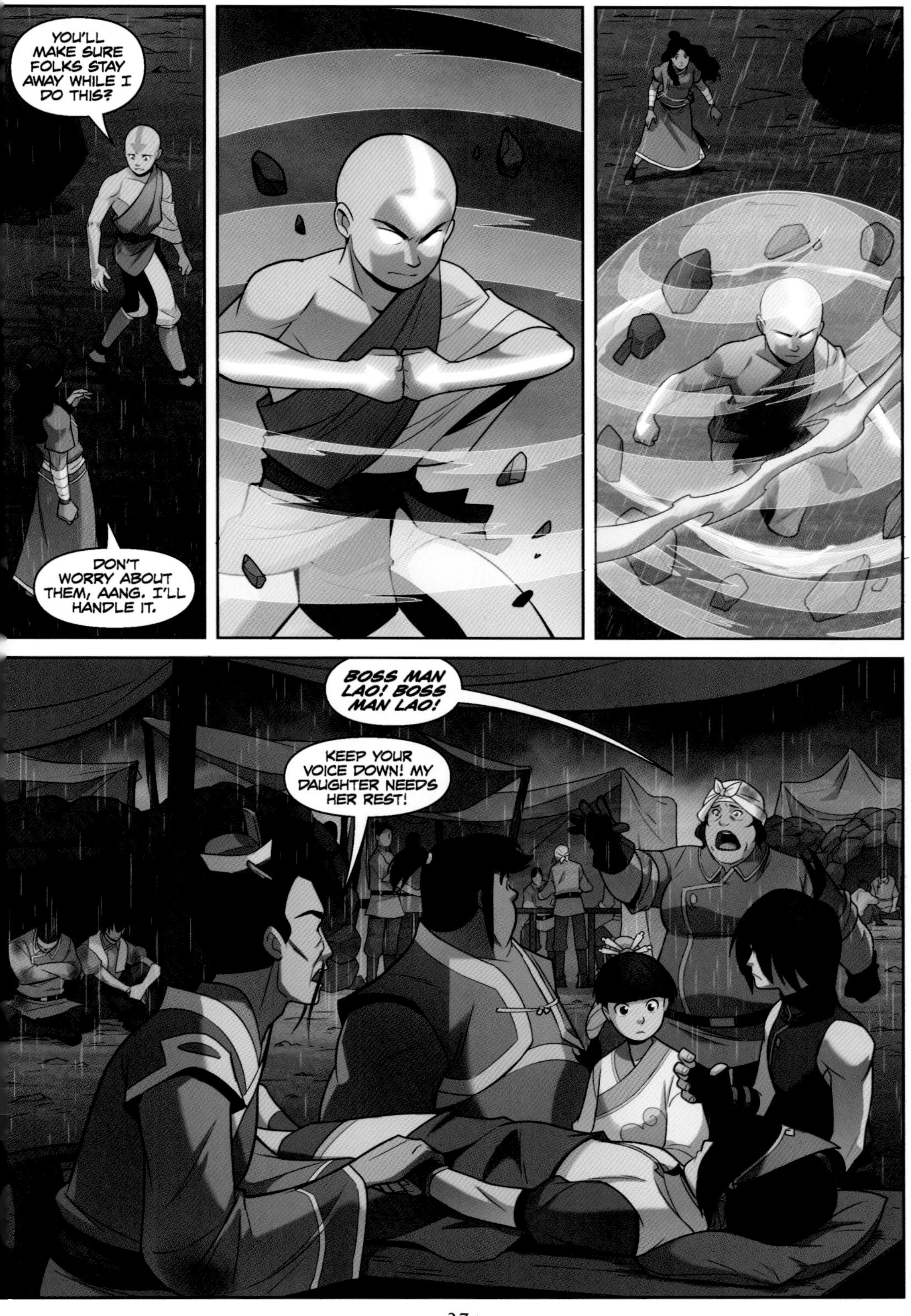
YOU'LL MAKE SURE FOLKS STAY AWAY WHILE I DO THIS?
DON'T WORRY ABOUT THEM, AANG. I'LL HANDLE IT.
BOSS MAN LAO! BOSS MAN LAO!
KEEP YOUR VOICE DOWN! MY DAUGHTER NEEDS HER REST!

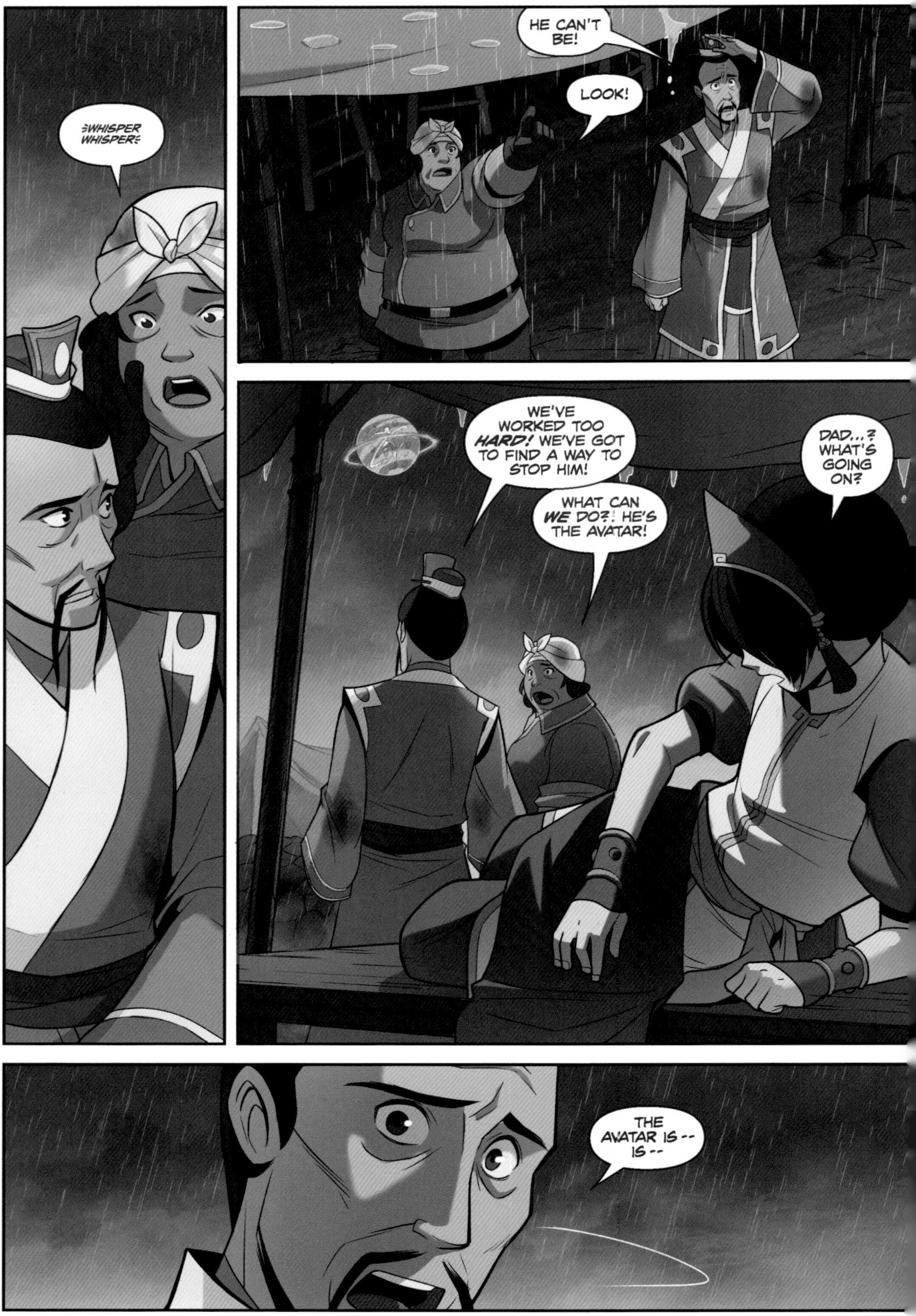

WHISPER WHISPER
HE CAN'T BE!
LOOK!
WE'VE WORKED TOO HARD! WE'VE GOT TO FIND A WAY TO STOP HIM!
WHAT CAN WE DO?! HE'S THE AVATAR!
DAD...? WHAT'S GOING ON?
THE AVATAR IS -- IS --

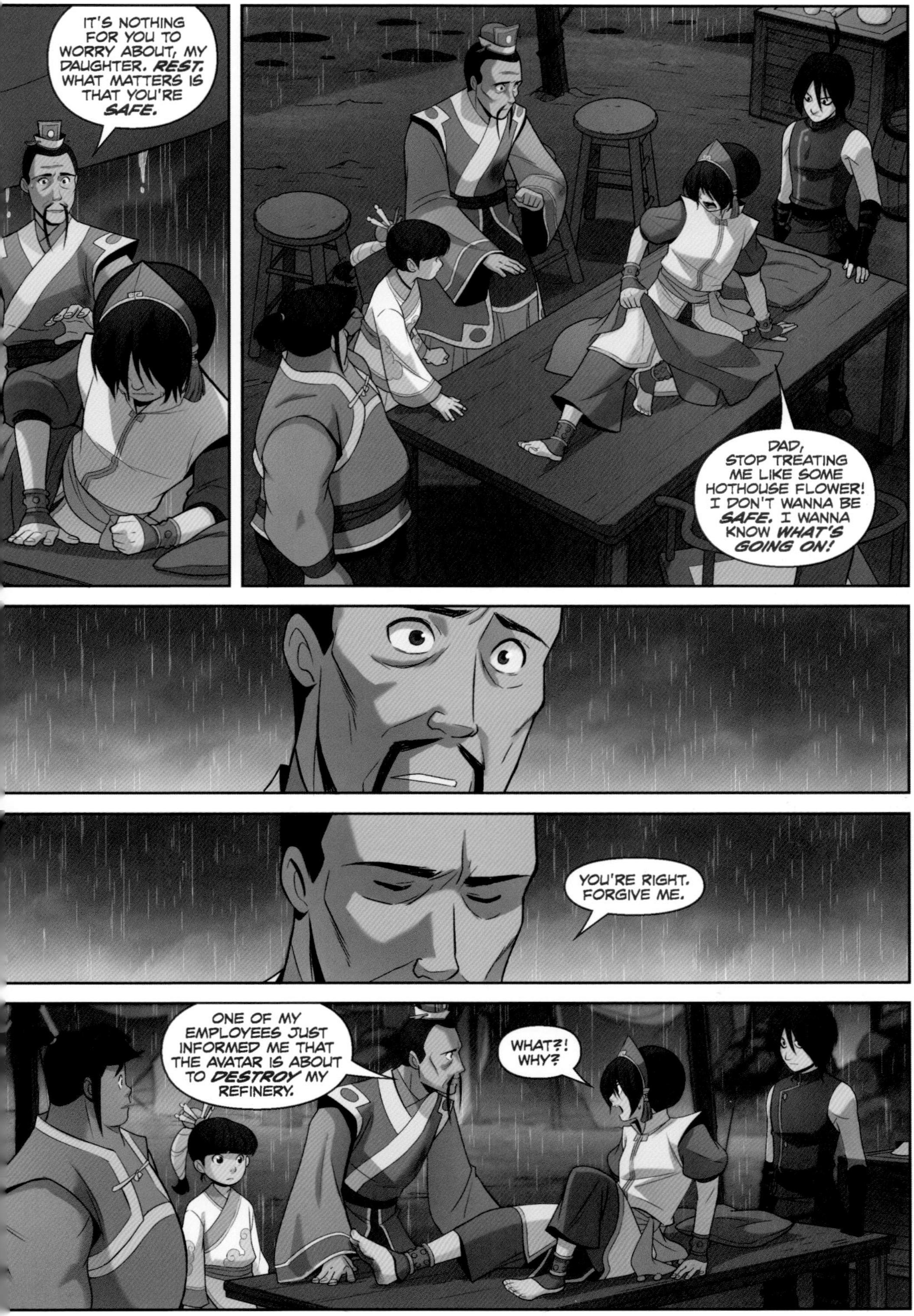
IT'S NOTHING FOR YOU TO WORRY ABOUT, MY DAUGHTER. REST. WHAT MATTERS IS THAT YOU'RE SAFE.
DAD, STOP TREATING ME LIKE SOME HOTHOUSE FLOWER! I DON'T WANNA BE SAFE. I WANNA KNOW WHAT'S GOING ON!
YOU'RE RIGHT. FORGIVE ME.
ONE OF MY EMPLOYEES JUST INFORMED ME THAT THE AVATAR IS ABOUT TO DESTROY MY REFINERY.
WHAT?! WHY?

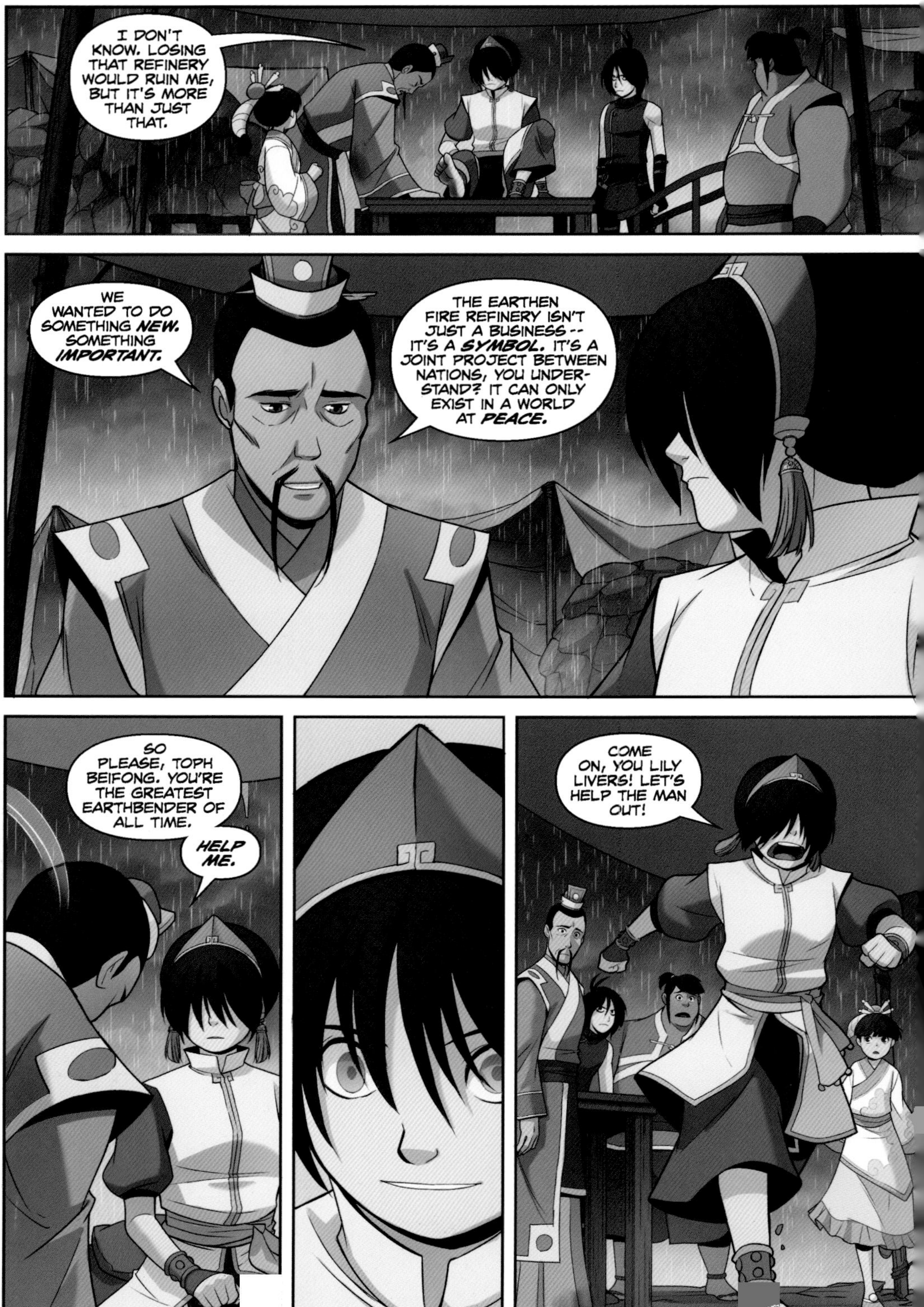
I DON'T KNOW. LOSING THAT REFINERY WOULD RUIN ME, BUT IT'S MORE THAN JUST THAT.
WE WANTED TO DO SOMETHING *NEW.* SOMETHING *IMPORTANT.*
THE EARTHEN FIRE REFINERY ISN'T JUST A BUSINESS -- IT'S A *SYMBOL.* IT'S A JOINT PROJECT BETWEEN NATIONS, YOU UNDER-STAND? IT CAN ONLY EXIST IN A WORLD AT *PEACE.*
SO PLEASE, TOPH BEIFONG. YOU'RE THE GREATEST EARTHBENDER OF ALL TIME.
HELP ME.
COME ON, YOU LILY LIVERS! LET'S HELP THE MAN OUT!

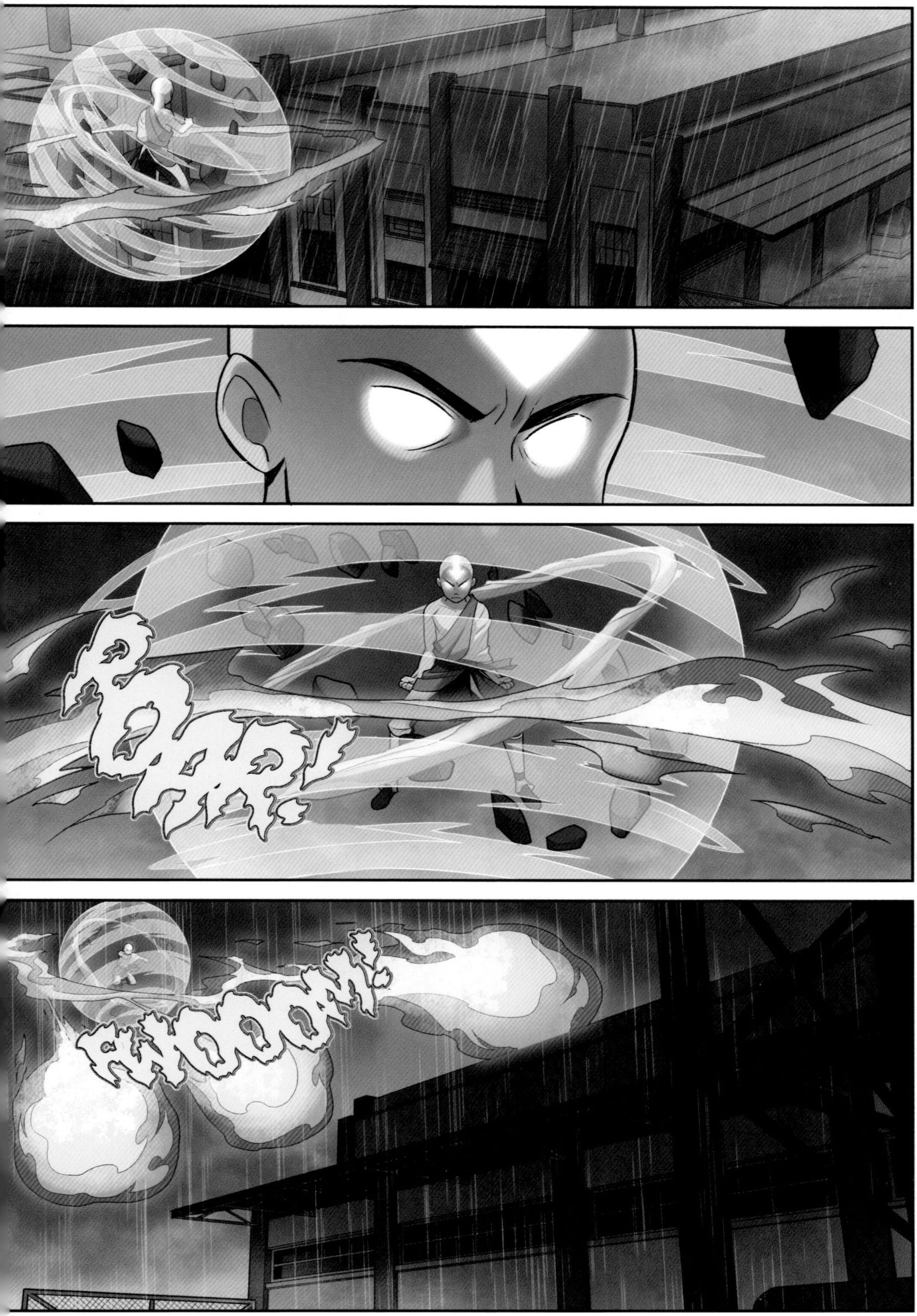
ROAR!
FWOOOM!

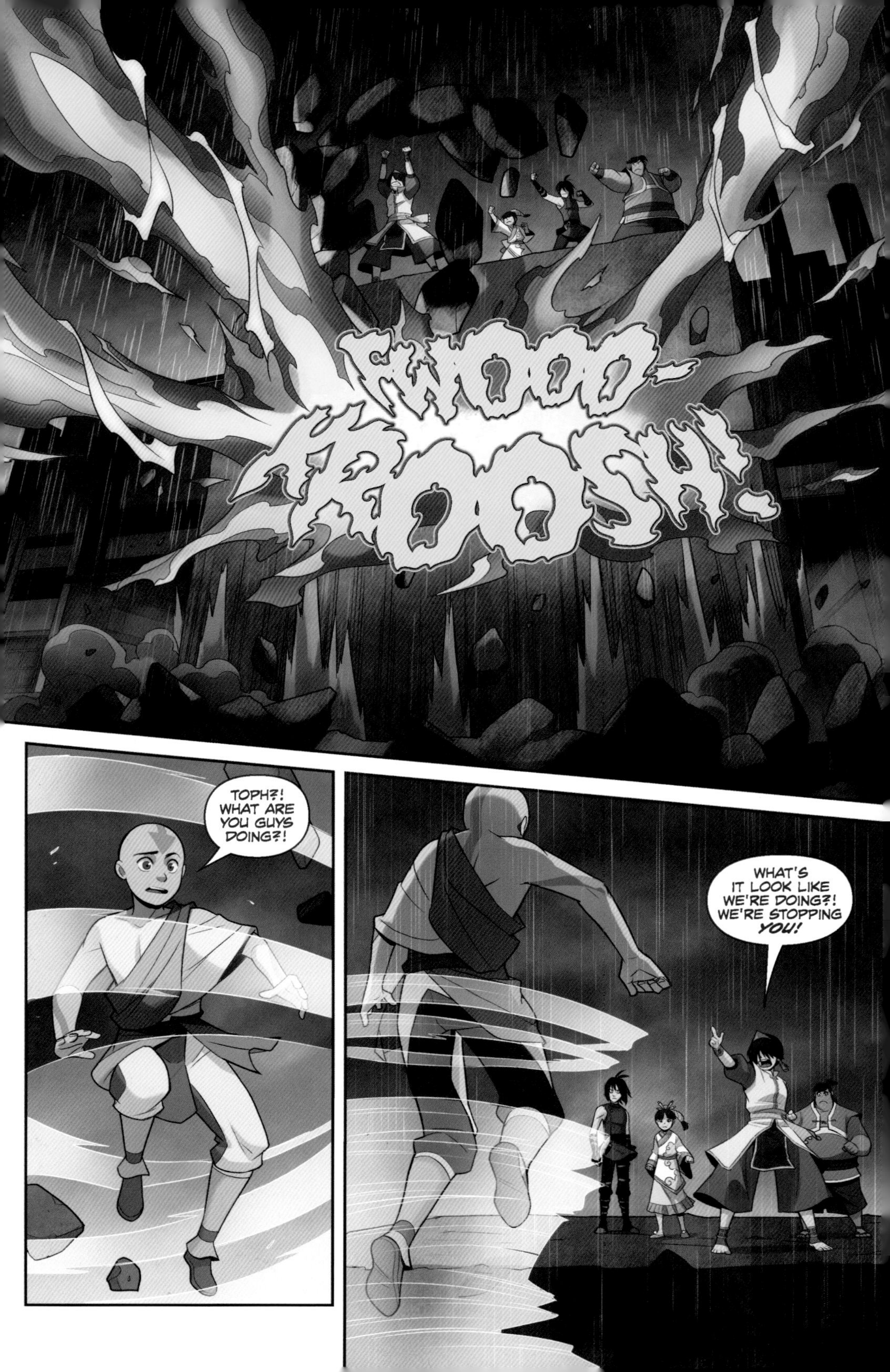
FWOOO-KROOSH!
TOPH?! WHAT ARE YOU GUYS DOING?!
WHAT'S IT LOOK LIKE WE'RE DOING?! WE'RE STOPPING *YOU!*

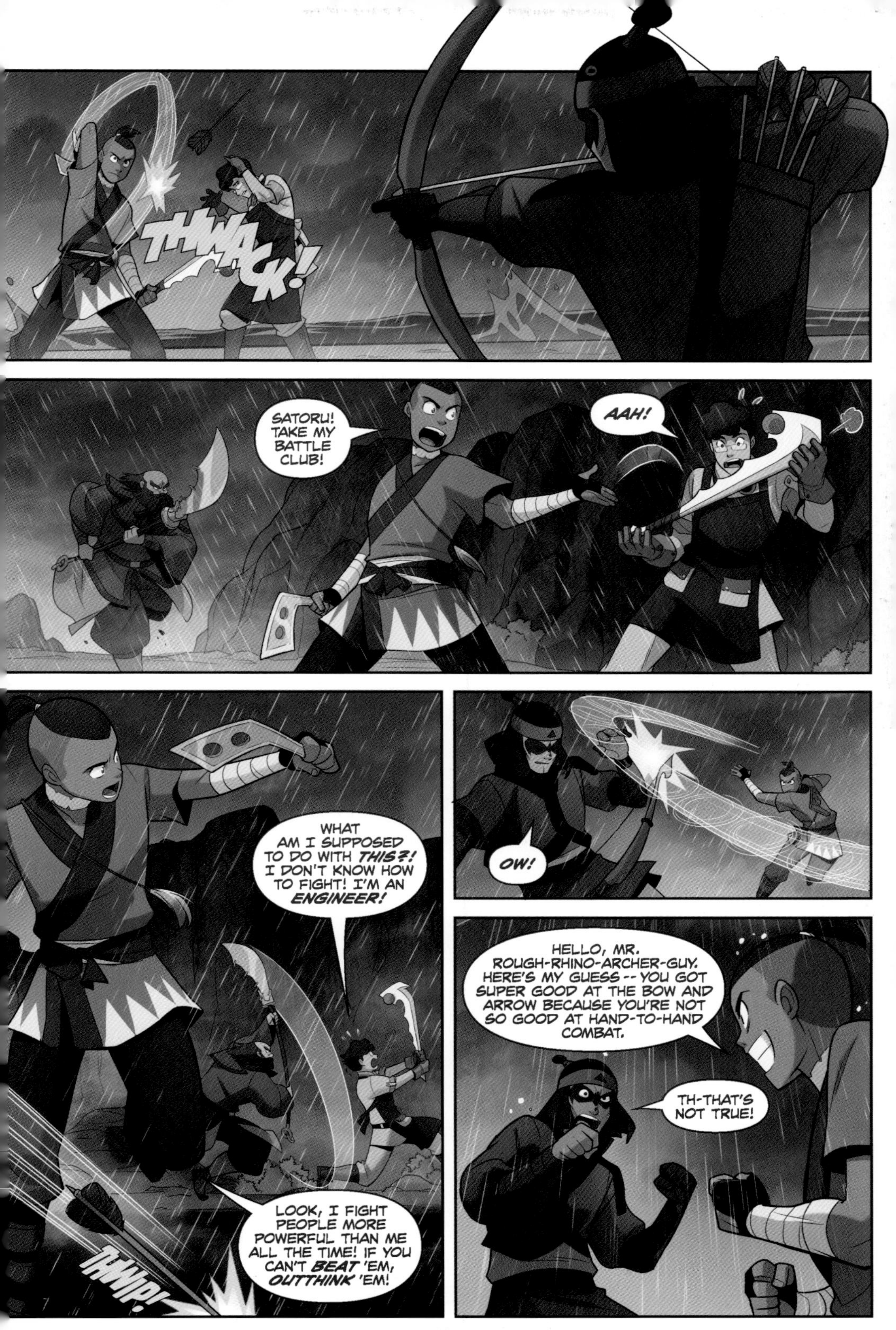
THWACK!
SATORU! TAKE MY BATTLE CLUB!
AAH!
WHAT AM I SUPPOSED TO DO WITH THIS?! I DON'T KNOW HOW TO FIGHT! I'M AN ENGINEER!
LOOK, I FIGHT PEOPLE MORE POWERFUL THAN ME ALL THE TIME! IF YOU CAN'T BEAT 'EM, OUTTHINK 'EM!
THWIP!
OW!
HELLO, MR. ROUGH-RHINO-ARCHER-GUY. HERE'S MY GUESS -- YOU GOT SUPER GOOD AT THE BOW AND ARROW BECAUSE YOU'RE NOT SO GOOD AT HAND-TO-HAND COMBAT.
TH-THAT'S NOT TRUE!

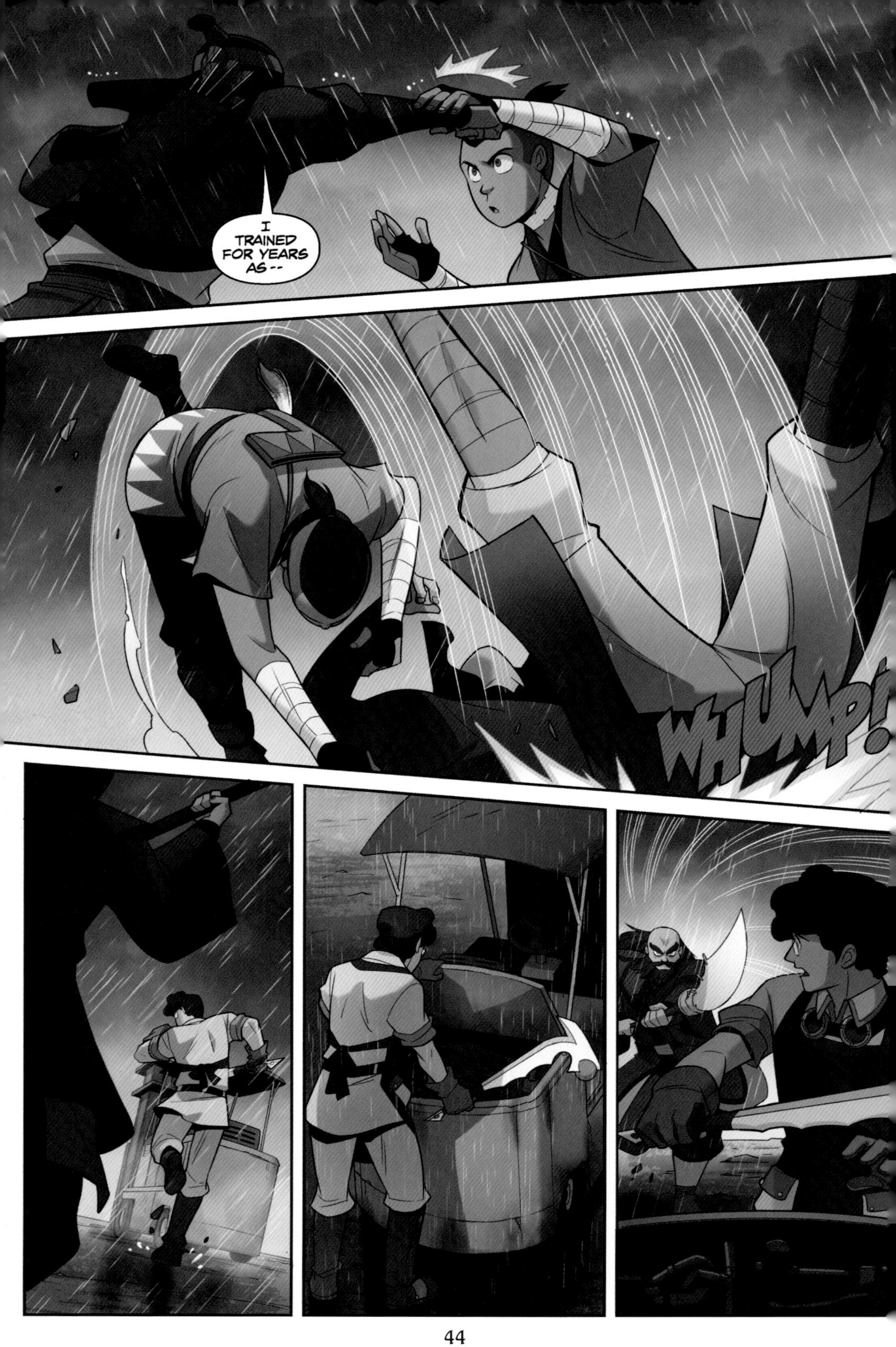
I TRAINED FOR YEARS AS --
WHUMP!

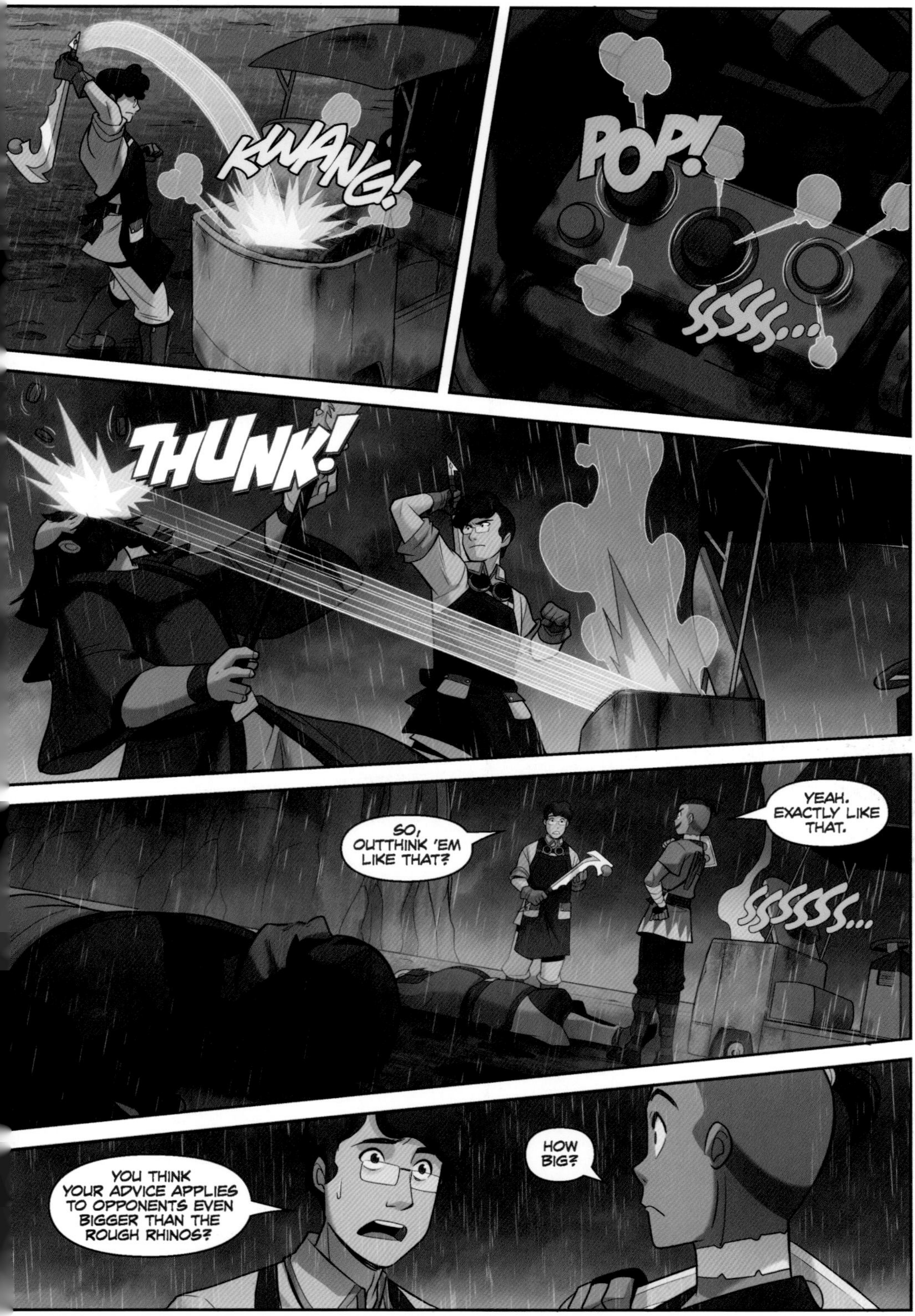
KWANG!
POP!
SSSSS...
THUNK!
SO, OUTTHINK 'EM LIKE THAT?
YEAH. EXACTLY LIKE THAT.
SSSSSS...
YOU THINK YOUR ADVICE APPLIES TO OPPONENTS EVEN BIGGER THAN THE ROUGH RHINOS?
HOW BIG?

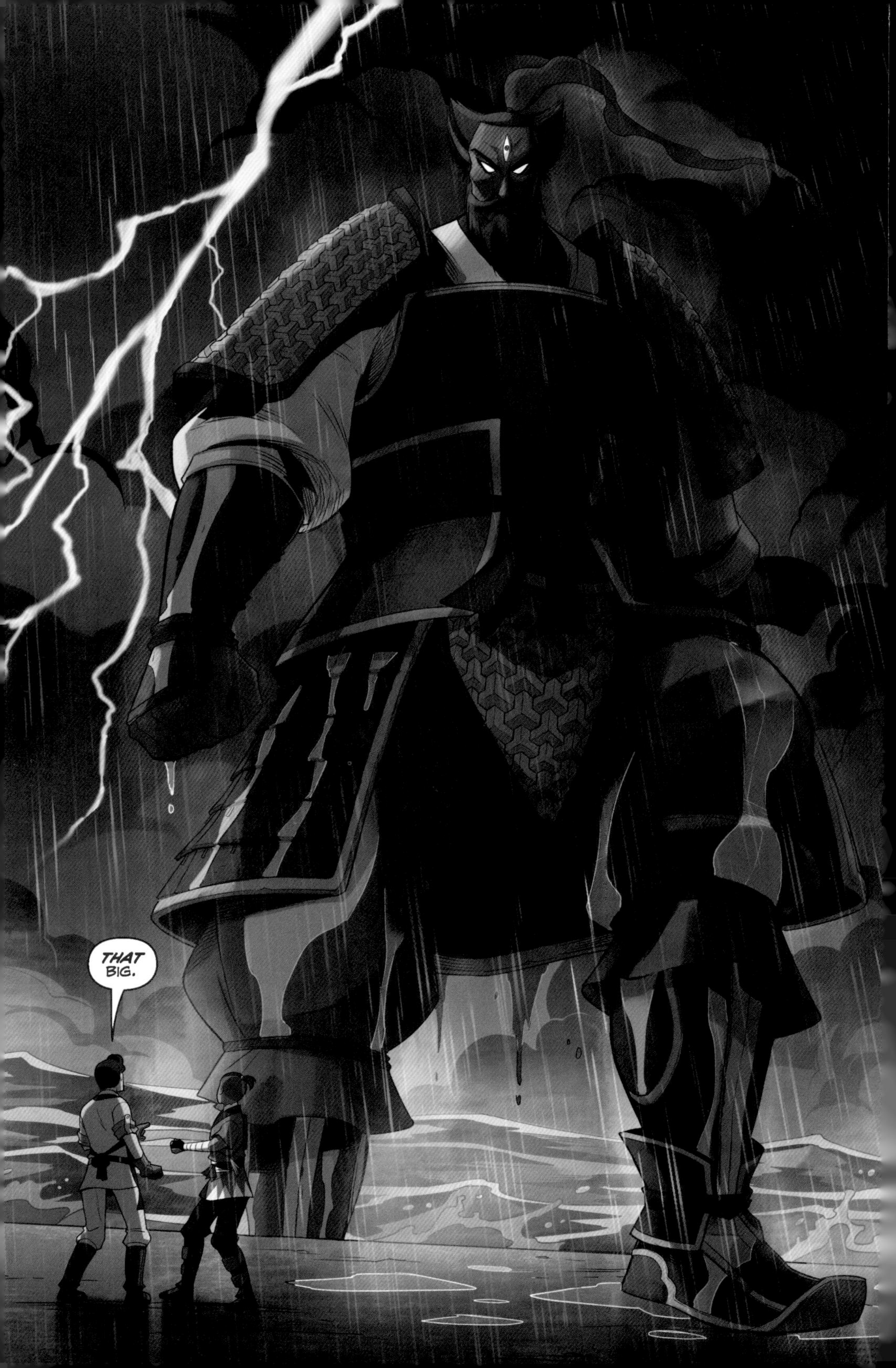
THAT BIG.

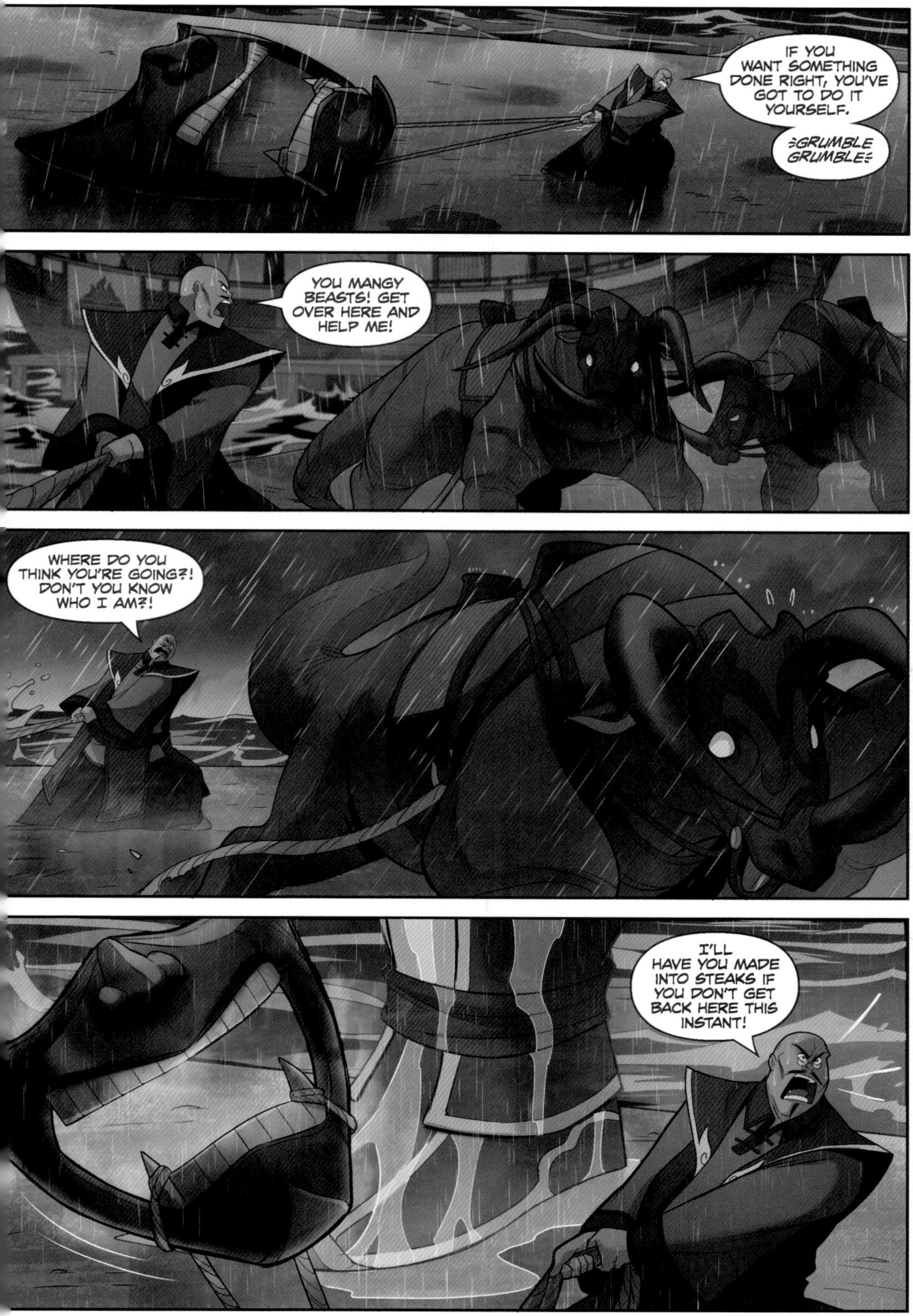
IF YOU WANT SOMETHING DONE RIGHT, YOU'VE GOT TO DO IT YOURSELF.
GRUMBLE GRUMBLE
YOU MANGY BEASTS! GET OVER HERE AND HELP ME!
WHERE DO YOU THINK YOU'RE GOING?! DON'T YOU KNOW WHO I AM?!
I'LL HAVE YOU MADE INTO STEAKS IF YOU DON'T GET BACK HERE THIS INSTANT!

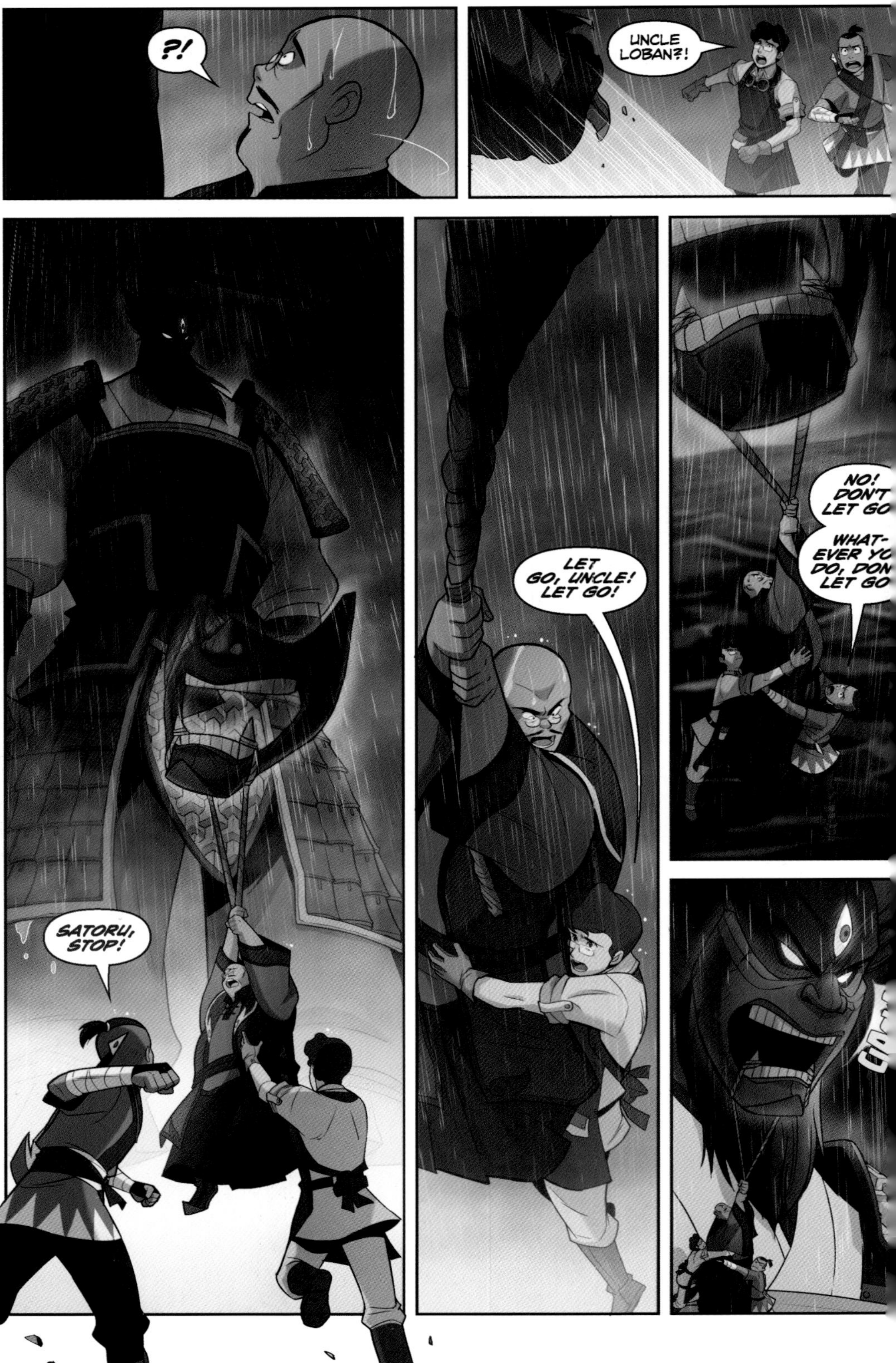
?!
UNCLE LOBAN?!
SATORU, STOP!
LET GO, UNCLE! LET GO!
NO! DON'T LET GO
WHAT-EVER YO DO, DON LET GO

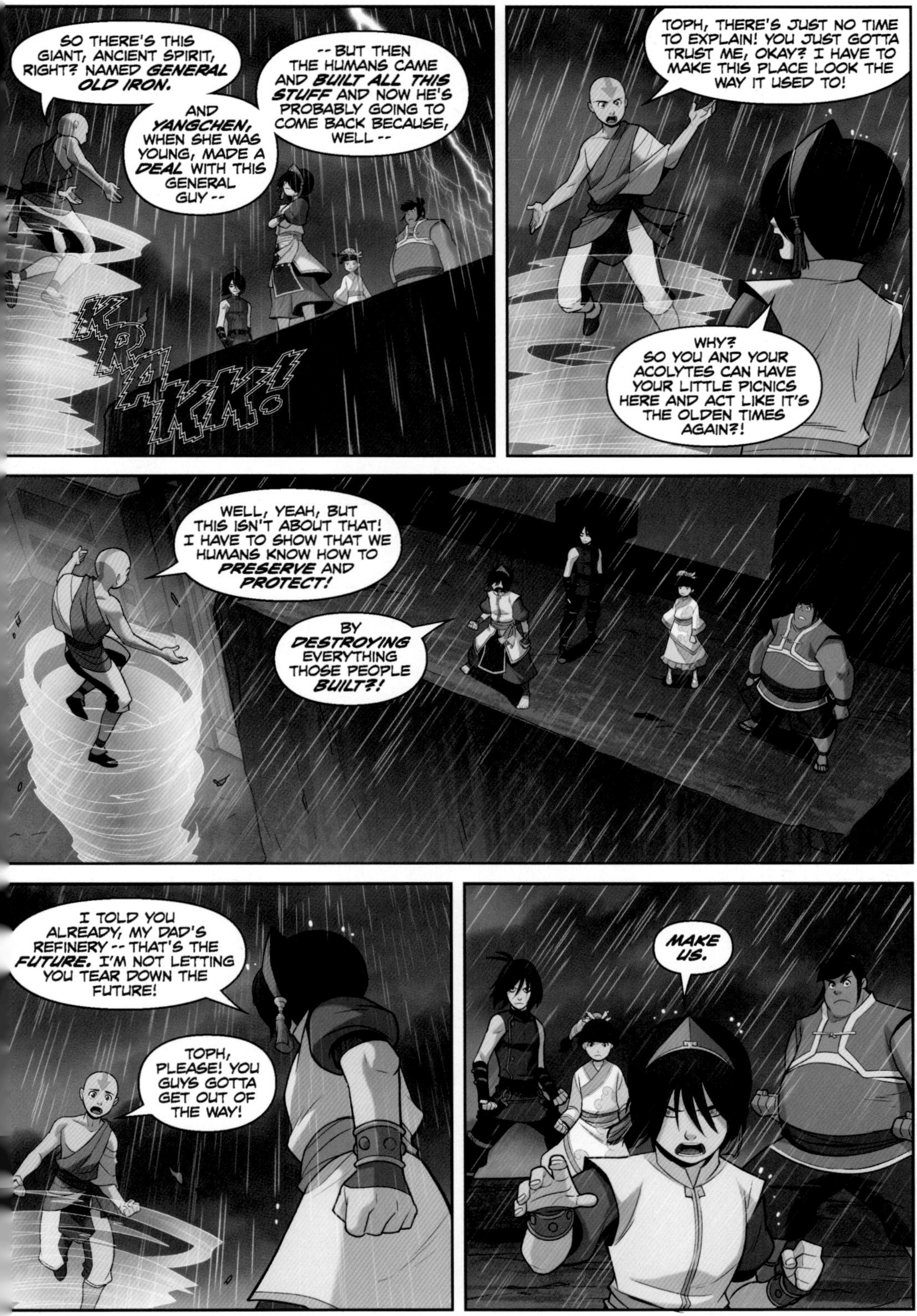
SO THERE'S THIS GIANT, ANCIENT SPIRIT, RIGHT? NAMED GENERAL OLD IRON.
AND YANGCHEN, WHEN SHE WAS YOUNG, MADE A DEAL WITH THIS GENERAL GUY --
-- BUT THEN THE HUMANS CAME AND BUILT ALL THIS STUFF AND NOW HE'S PROBABLY GOING TO COME BACK BECAUSE, WELL --
KRAKKA!
TOPH, THERE'S JUST NO TIME TO EXPLAIN! YOU JUST GOTTA TRUST ME, OKAY? I HAVE TO MAKE THIS PLACE LOOK THE WAY IT USED TO!
WHY? SO YOU AND YOUR ACOLYTES CAN HAVE YOUR LITTLE PICNICS HERE AND ACT LIKE IT'S THE OLDEN TIMES AGAIN?!
WELL, YEAH, BUT THIS ISN'T ABOUT THAT! I HAVE TO SHOW THAT WE HUMANS KNOW HOW TO PRESERVE AND PROTECT!
BY DESTROYING EVERYTHING THOSE PEOPLE BUILT?!
I TOLD YOU ALREADY, MY DAD'S REFINERY -- THAT'S THE FUTURE. I'M NOT LETTING YOU TEAR DOWN THE FUTURE!
TOPH, PLEASE! YOU GUYS GOTTA GET OUT OF THE WAY!
MAKE US.

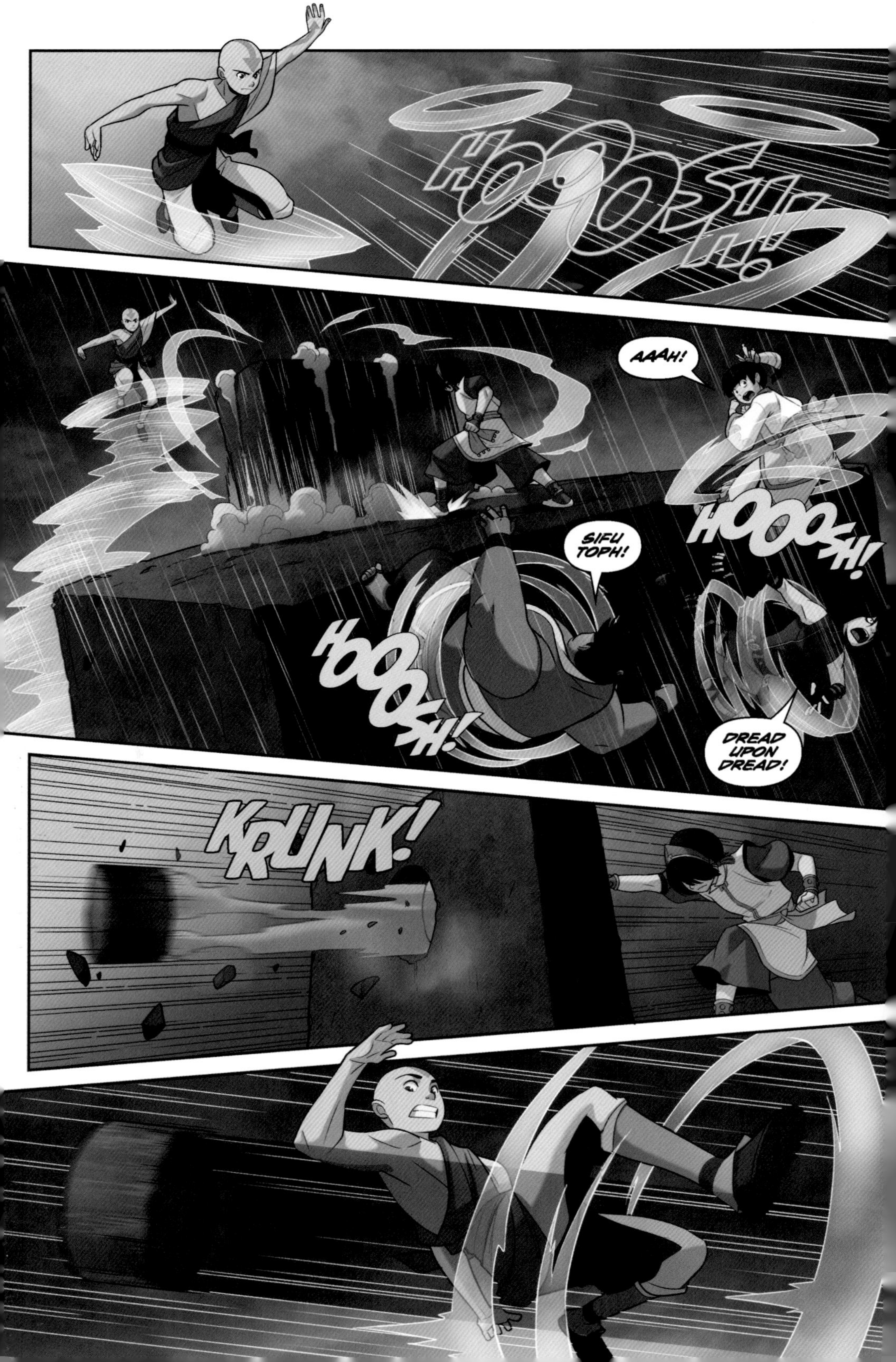
HOOOOSH!
AAAH!
SIFU TOPH!
HOOOSH!
HOOOSH!
DREAD UPON DREAD!
KRUNK!

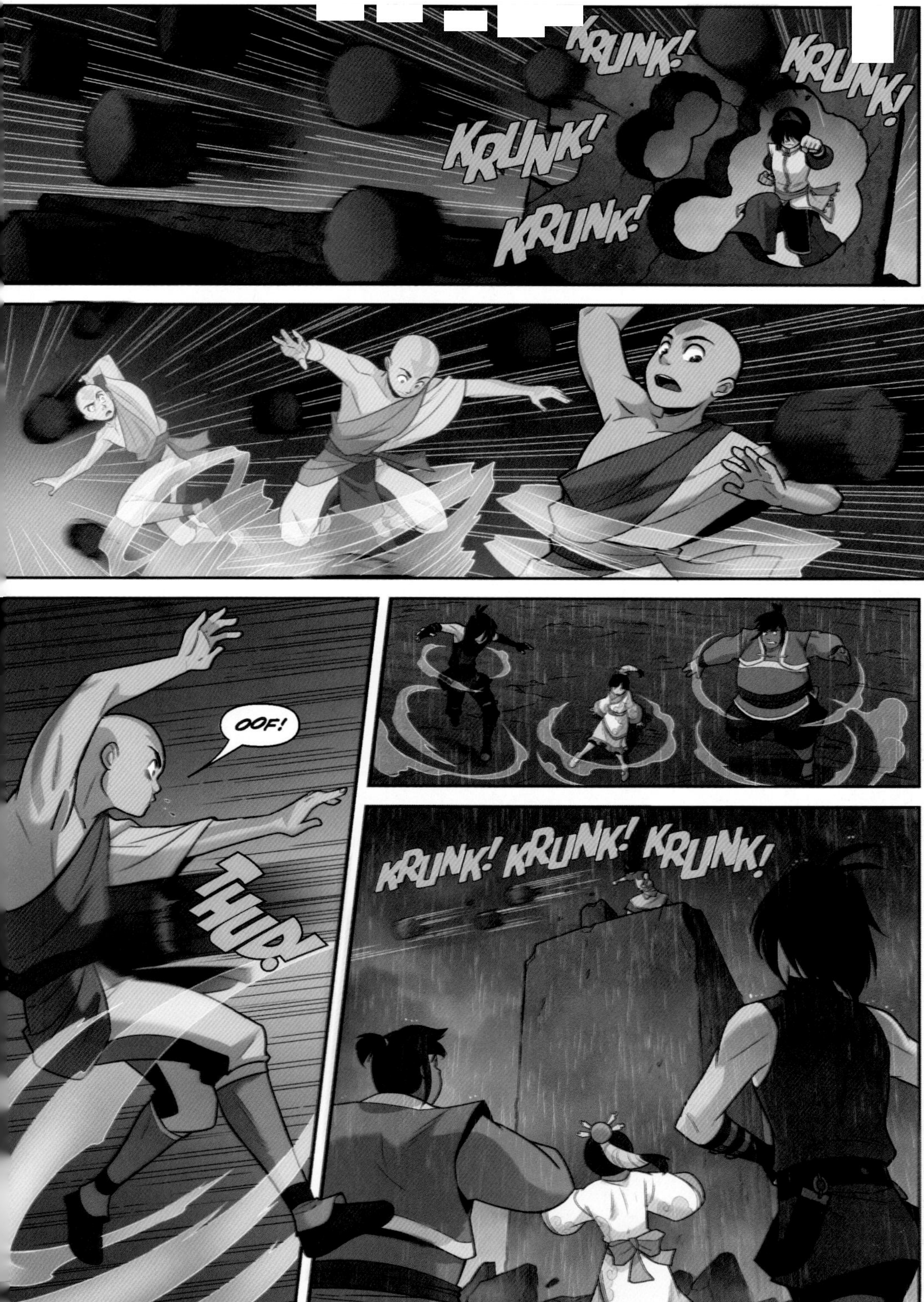
KRUNK!
KRUNK!
KRUNK!
KRUNK!
OOF!
THUD!
KRUNK! KRUNK! KRUNK!

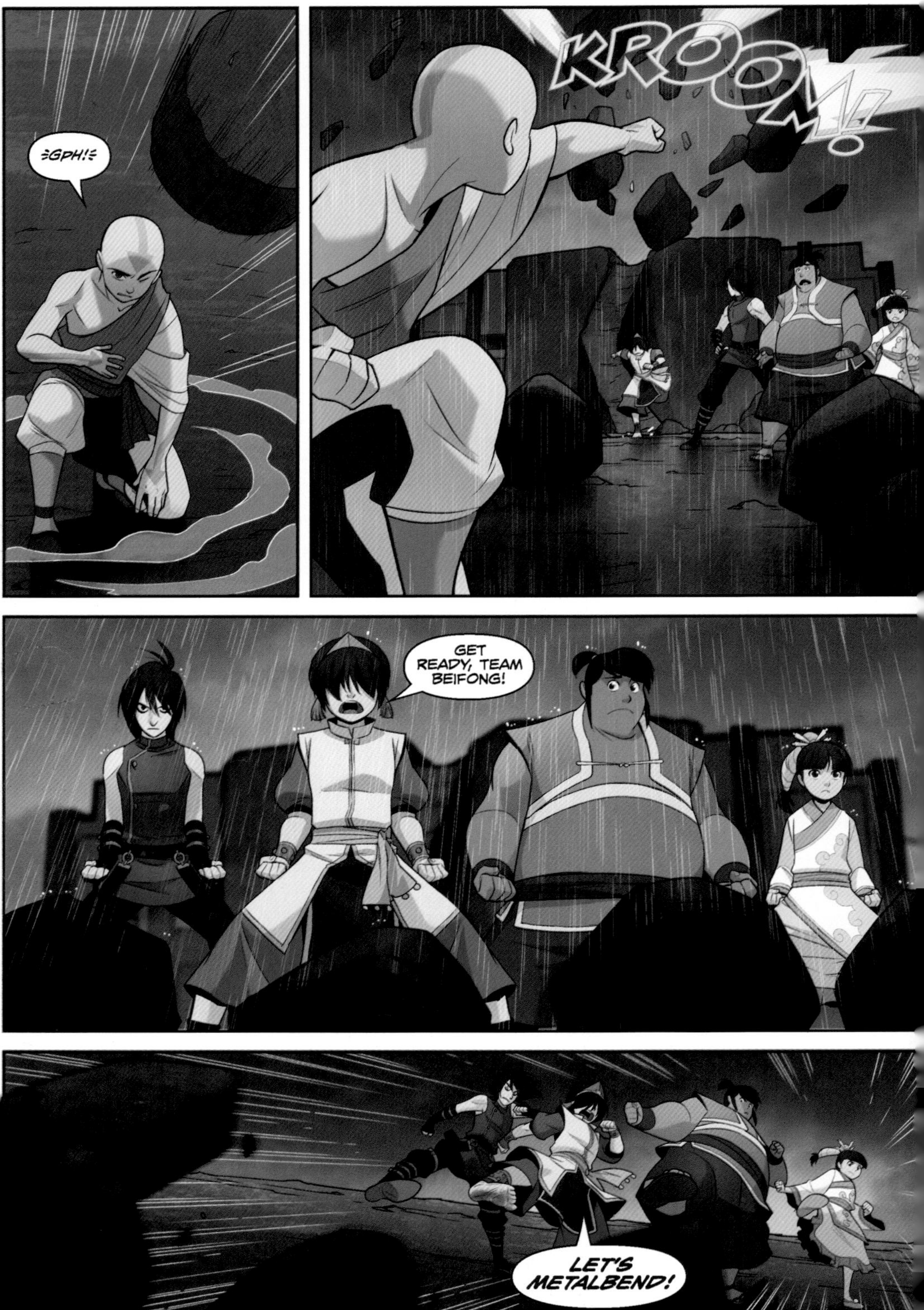
GPH!
KROOM!!
GET READY, TEAM BEIFONG!
LET'S METALBEND!

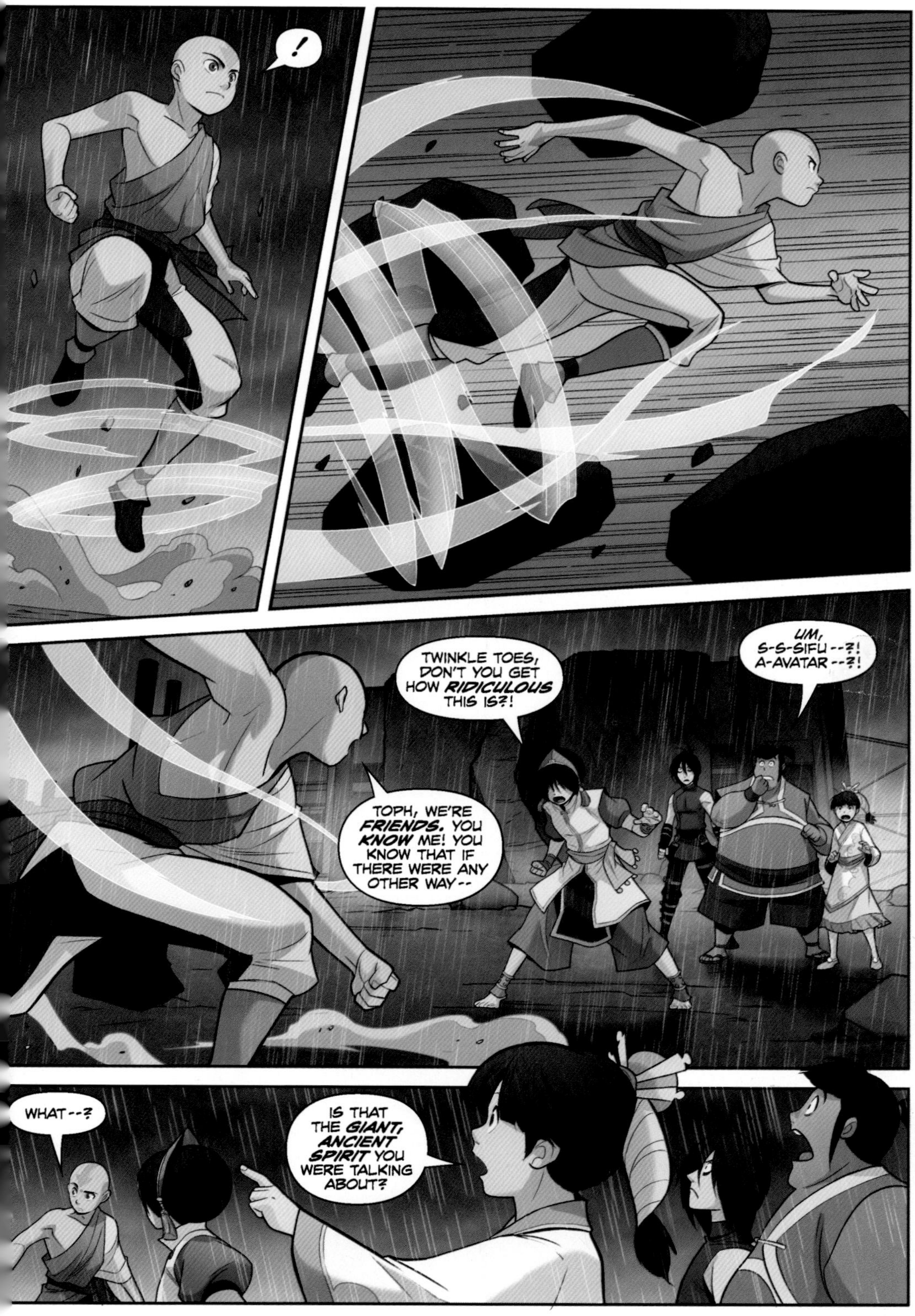
!
TWINKLE TOES, DON'T YOU GET HOW *RIDICULOUS* THIS IS?!
UM, S-S-SIFU--?! A-AVATAR--?!
TOPH, WE'RE *FRIENDS.* YOU *KNOW* ME! YOU KNOW THAT IF THERE WERE ANY OTHER WAY--
WHAT--?
IS THAT THE *GIANT, ANCIENT SPIRIT* YOU WERE TALKING ABOUT?

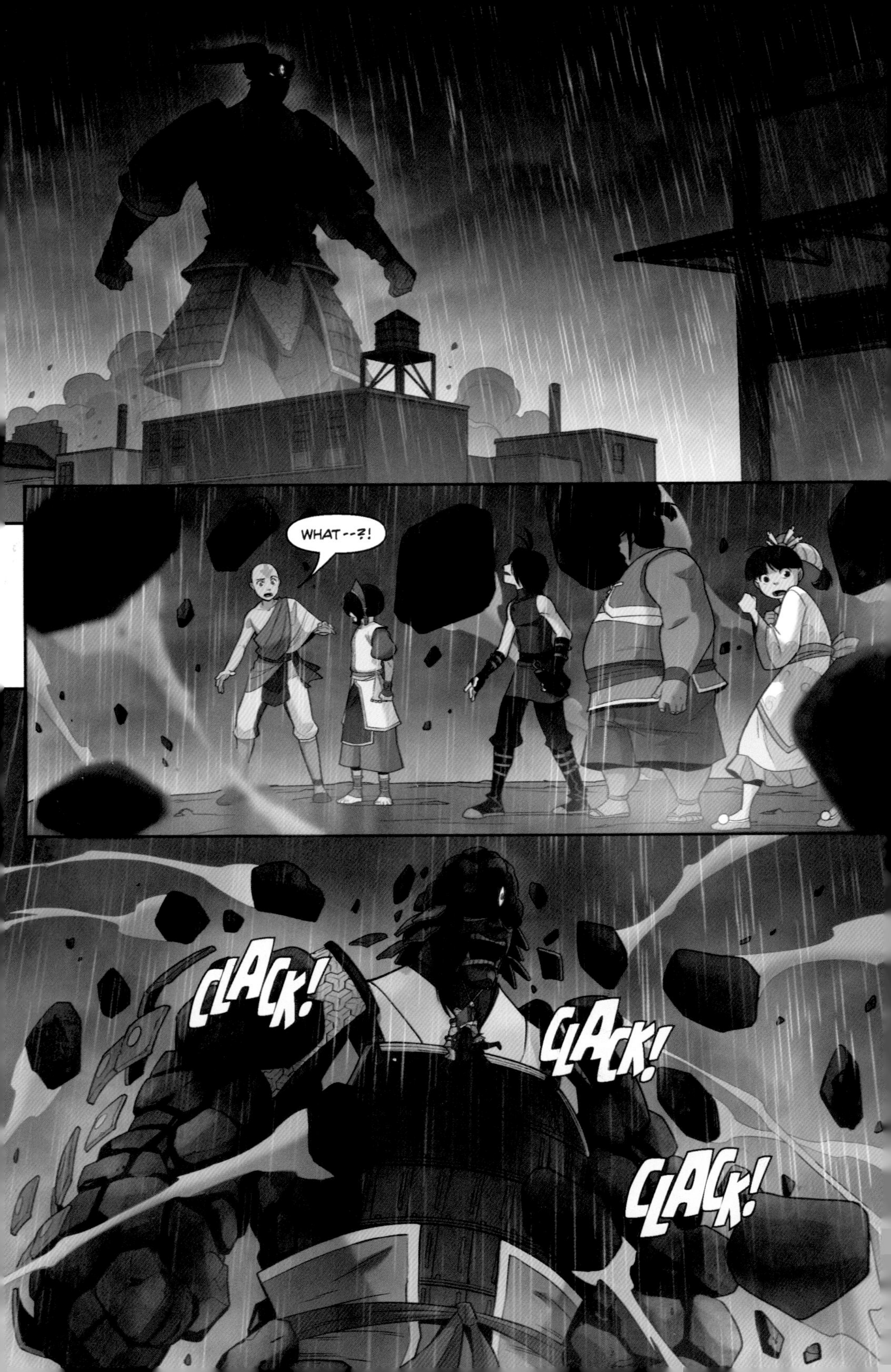
WHAT--?!
CLACK!
CLACK!
CLACK!

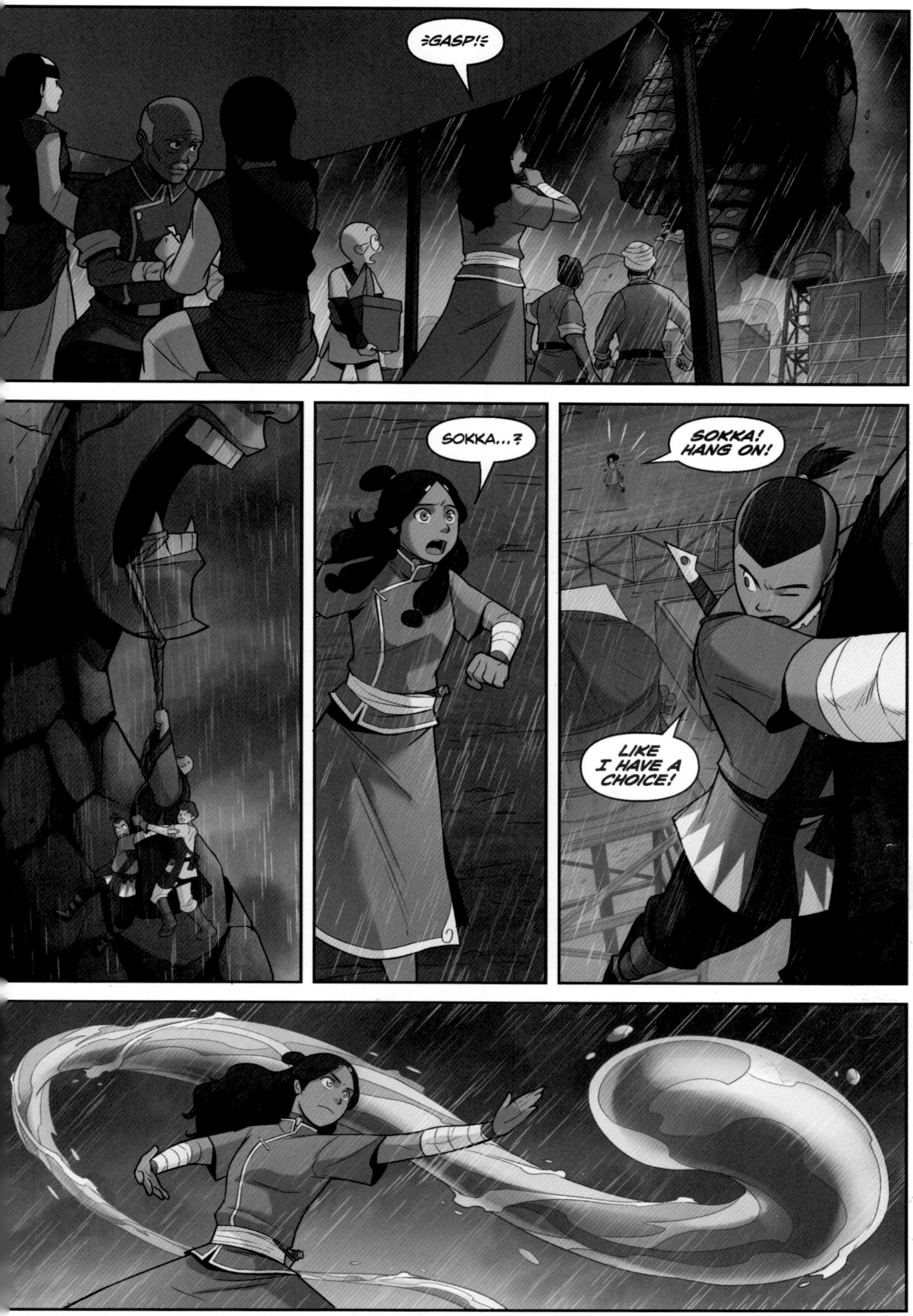
:GASP!:
SOKKA...?
SOKKA! HANG ON!
LIKE I HAVE A CHOICE!

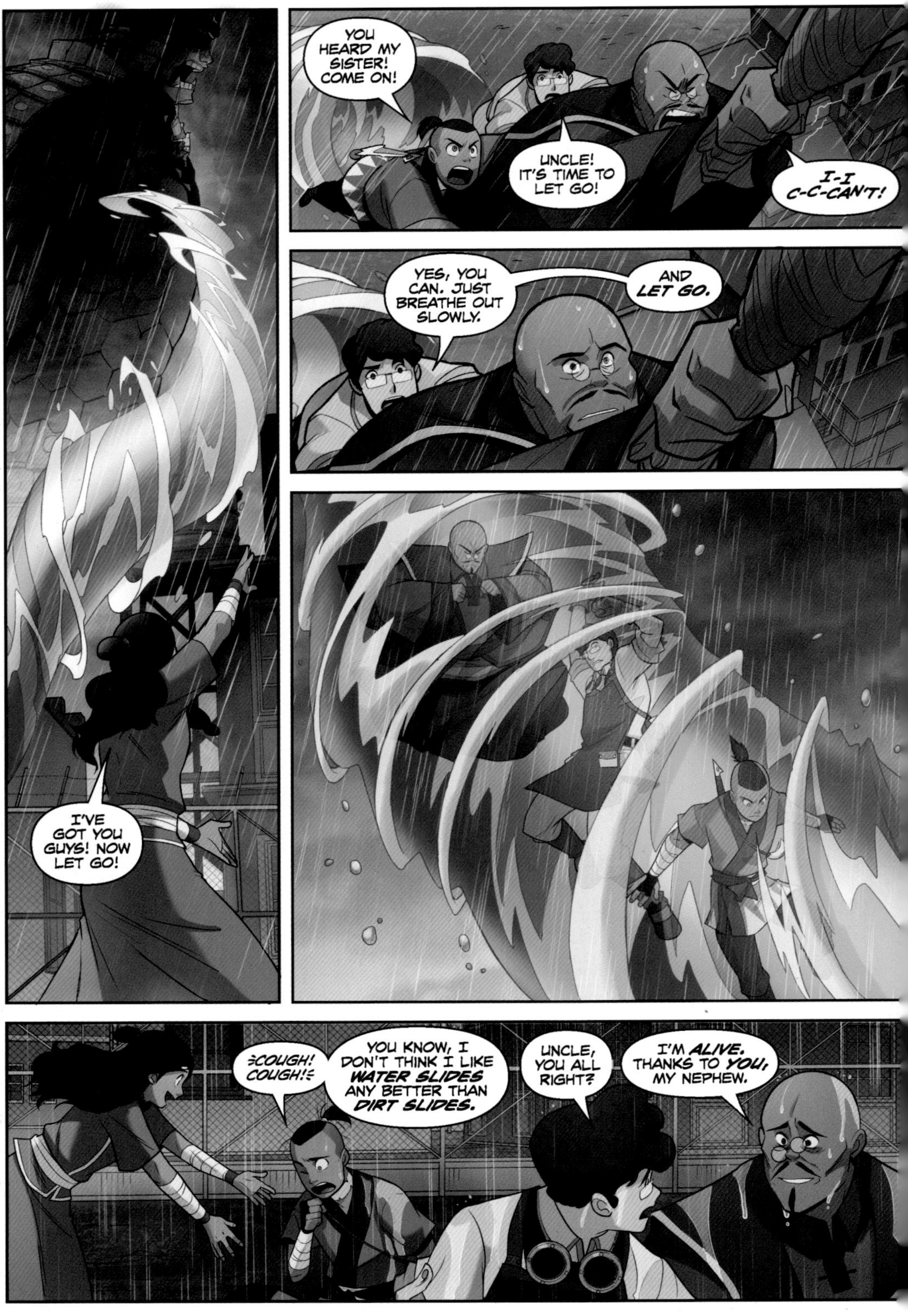
YOU HEARD MY SISTER! COME ON!
UNCLE! IT'S TIME TO LET GO!
I-I C-C-CAN'T!
YES, YOU CAN. JUST BREATHE OUT SLOWLY.
AND LET GO.
I'VE GOT YOU GUYS! NOW LET GO!
COUGH! COUGH!
YOU KNOW, I DON'T THINK I LIKE WATER SLIDES ANY BETTER THAN DIRT SLIDES.
UNCLE, YOU ALL RIGHT?
I'M ALIVE. THANKS TO YOU, MY NEPHEW.

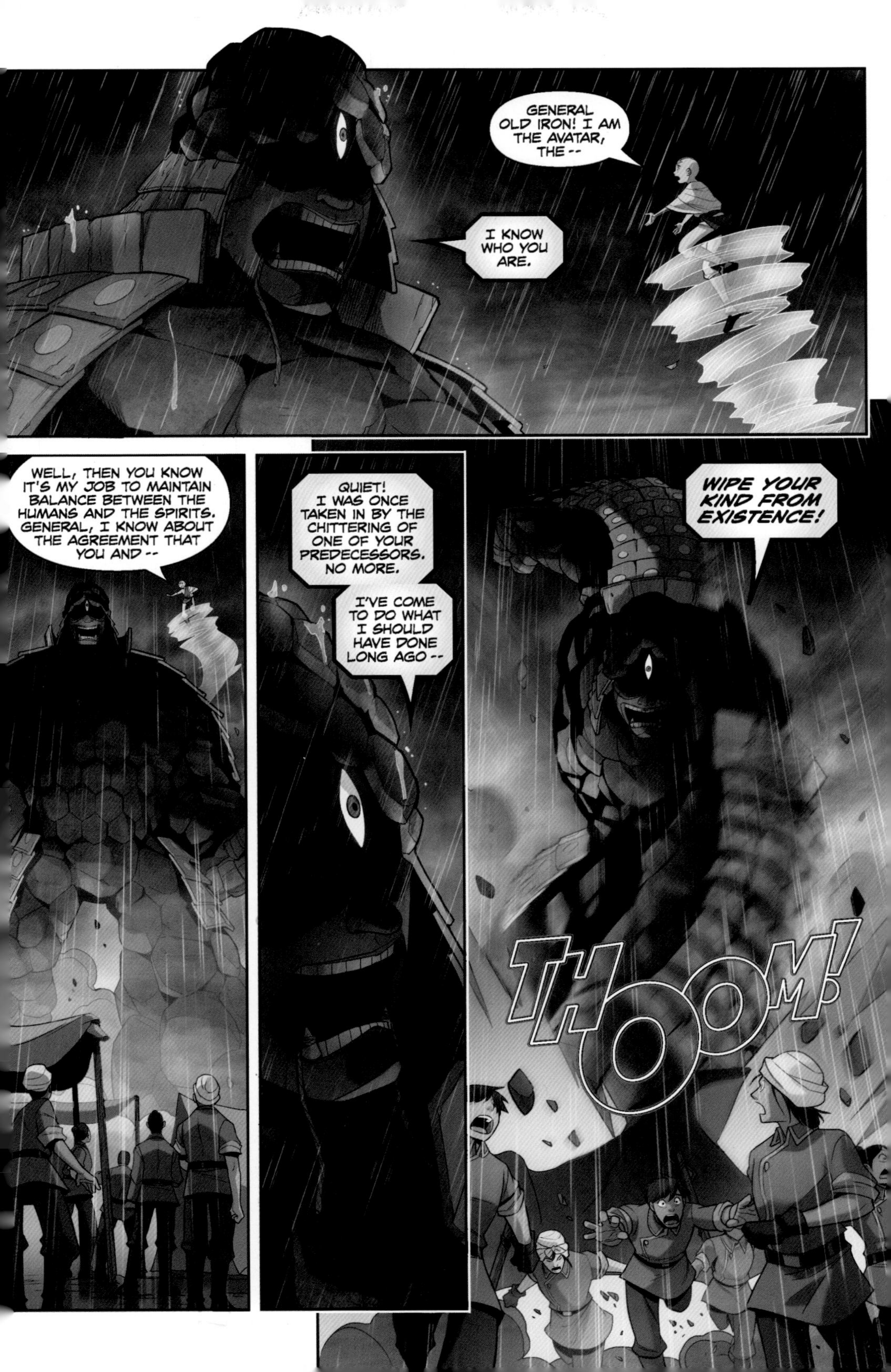
GENERAL OLD IRON! I AM THE AVATAR, THE --
I KNOW WHO YOU ARE.
WELL, THEN YOU KNOW IT'S MY JOB TO MAINTAIN BALANCE BETWEEN THE HUMANS AND THE SPIRITS. GENERAL, I KNOW ABOUT THE AGREEMENT THAT YOU AND --
QUIET! I WAS ONCE TAKEN IN BY THE CHITTERING OF ONE OF YOUR PREDECESSORS. NO MORE.
I'VE COME TO DO WHAT I SHOULD HAVE DONE LONG AGO --
WIPE YOUR KIND FROM EXISTENCE!
THOOOM!

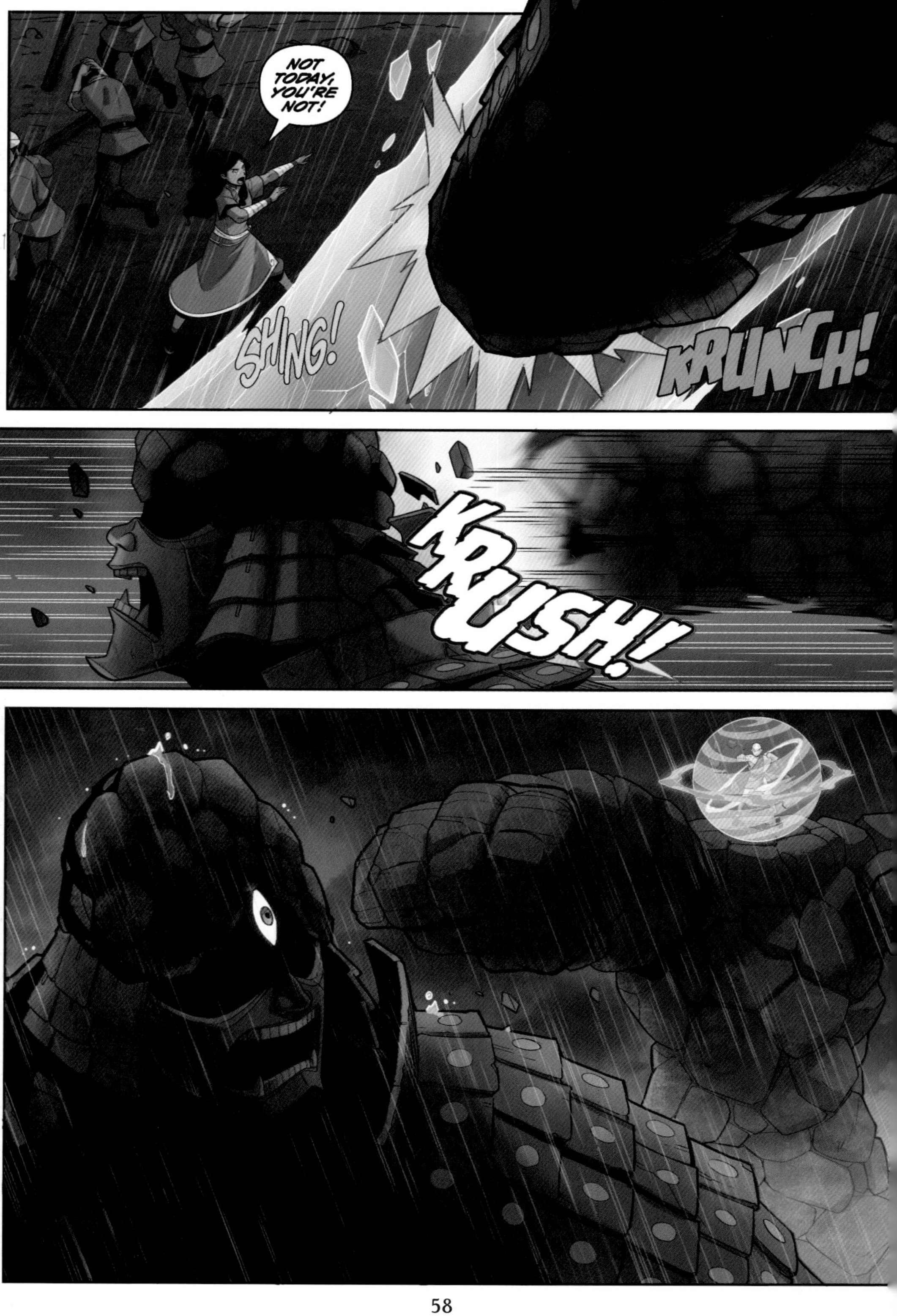
NOT TODAY, YOU'RE NOT!
SHING!
KRUNCH!
KRUSH!

KRACK!

KRACK!

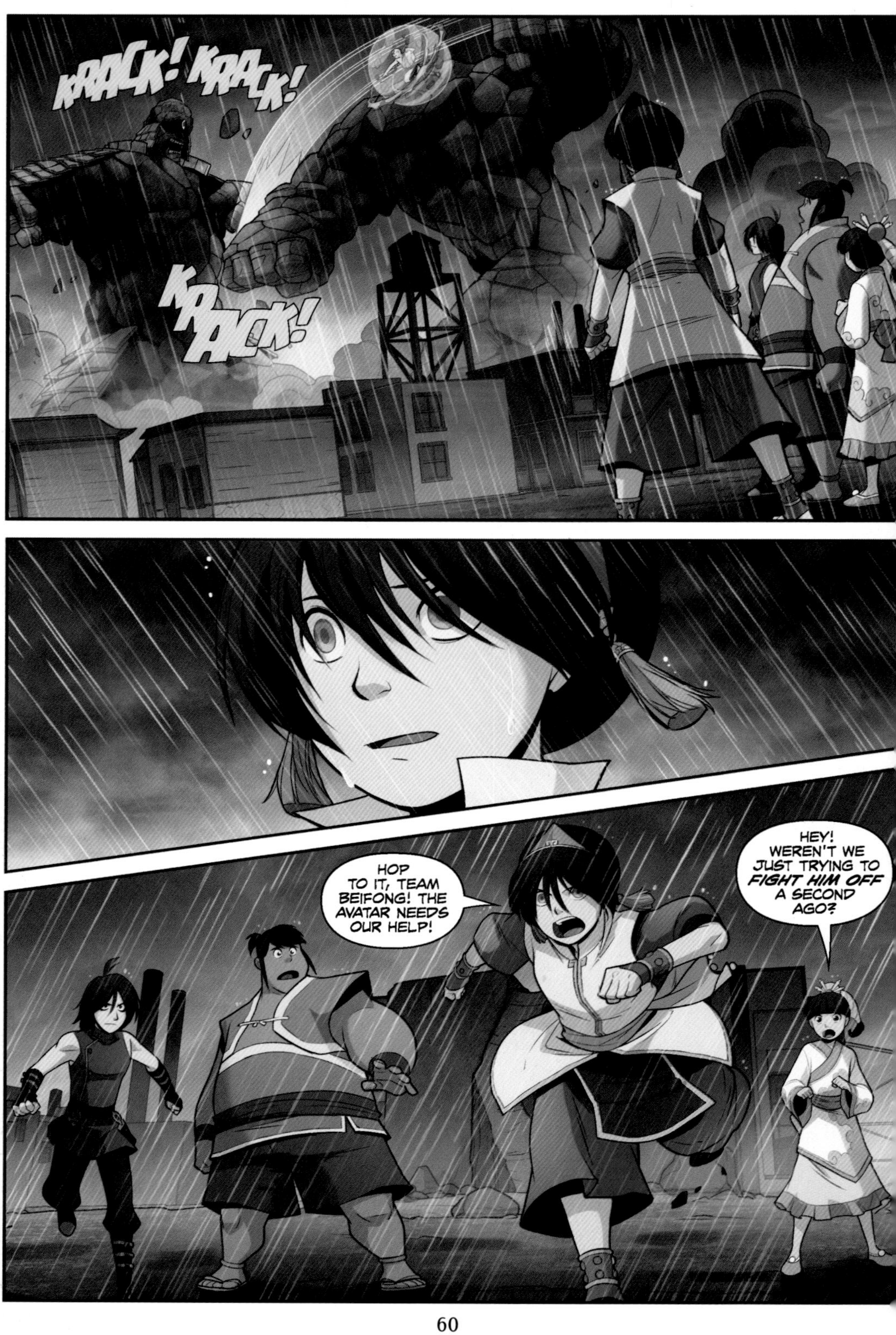
KRACK! KRACK!
KRAACK!
HOP TO IT, TEAM BEIFONG! THE AVATAR NEEDS OUR HELP!
HEY! WEREN'T WE JUST TRYING TO FIGHT HIM OFF A SECOND AGO?

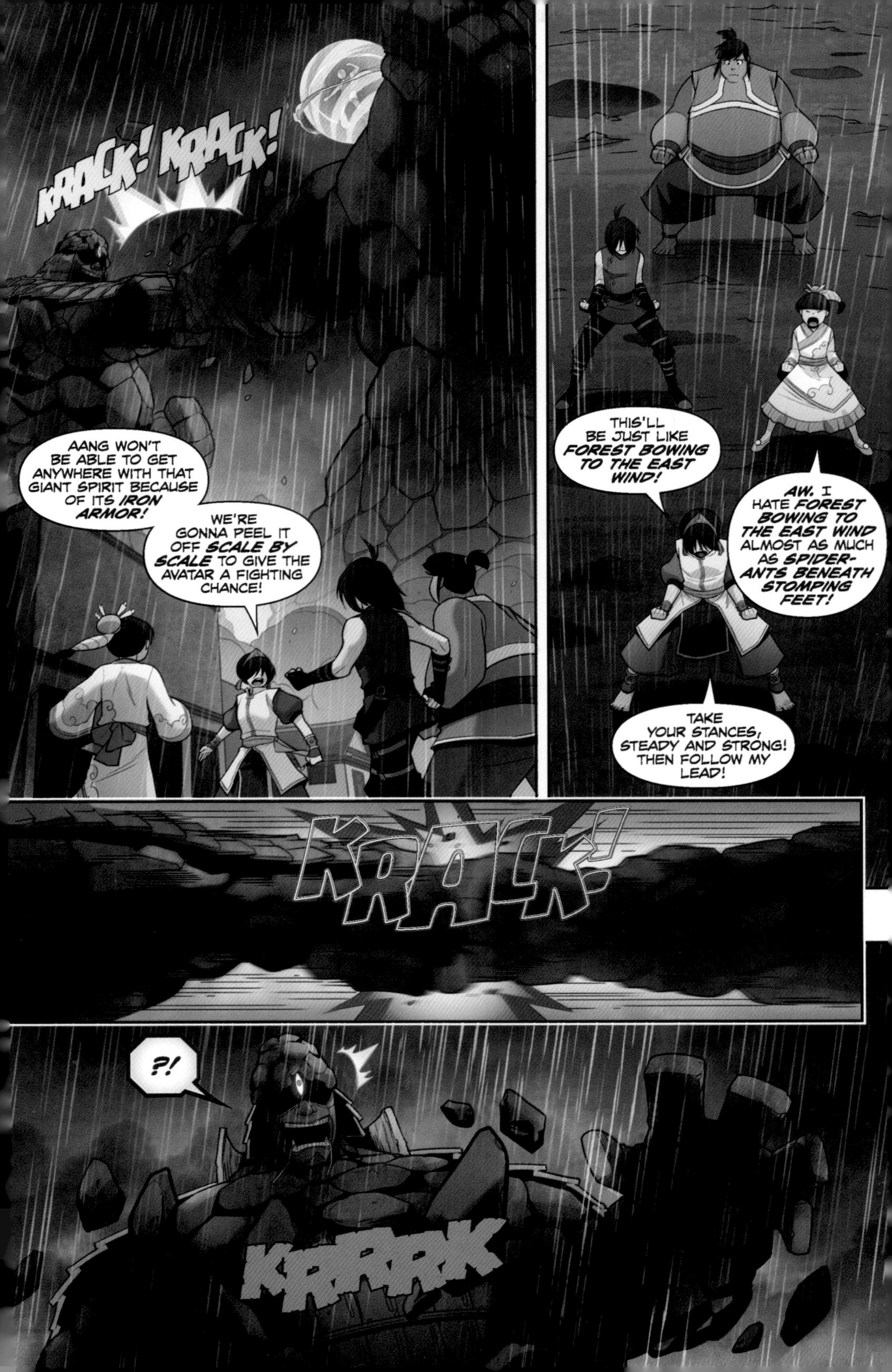
KRACK! KRACK!
AANG WON'T BE ABLE TO GET ANYWHERE WITH THAT GIANT SPIRIT BECAUSE OF ITS IRON ARMOR!
WE'RE GONNA PEEL IT OFF SCALE BY SCALE TO GIVE THE AVATAR A FIGHTING CHANCE!
THIS'LL BE JUST LIKE FOREST BOWING TO THE EAST WIND!
AW. I HATE FOREST BOWING TO THE EAST WIND ALMOST AS MUCH AS SPIDER-ANTS BENEATH STOMPING FEET!
TAKE YOUR STANCES, STEADY AND STRONG! THEN FOLLOW MY LEAD!
KRACK!
?!
KRRRK

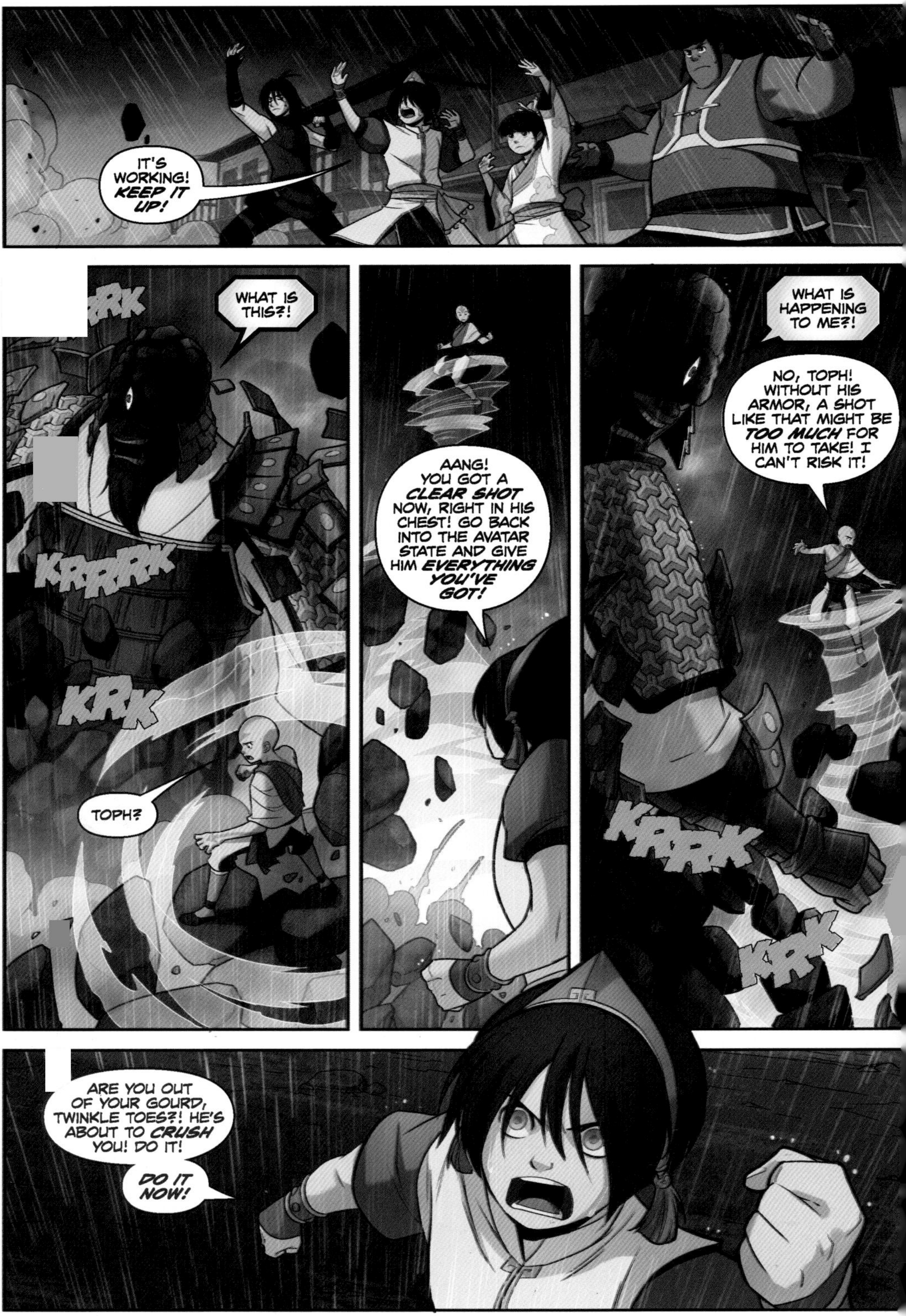
IT'S WORKING! KEEP IT UP!
KRRRK
WHAT IS THIS?!
KRRRK
KRK
TOPH?
AANG! YOU GOT A CLEAR SHOT NOW, RIGHT IN HIS CHEST! GO BACK INTO THE AVATAR STATE AND GIVE HIM EVERYTHING YOU'VE GOT!
WHAT IS HAPPENING TO ME?!
NO, TOPH! WITHOUT HIS ARMOR, A SHOT LIKE THAT MIGHT BE TOO MUCH FOR HIM TO TAKE! I CAN'T RISK IT!
KRRRK
KRK
ARE YOU OUT OF YOUR GOURD, TWINKLE TOES?! HE'S ABOUT TO CRUSH YOU! DO IT!
DO IT NOW!

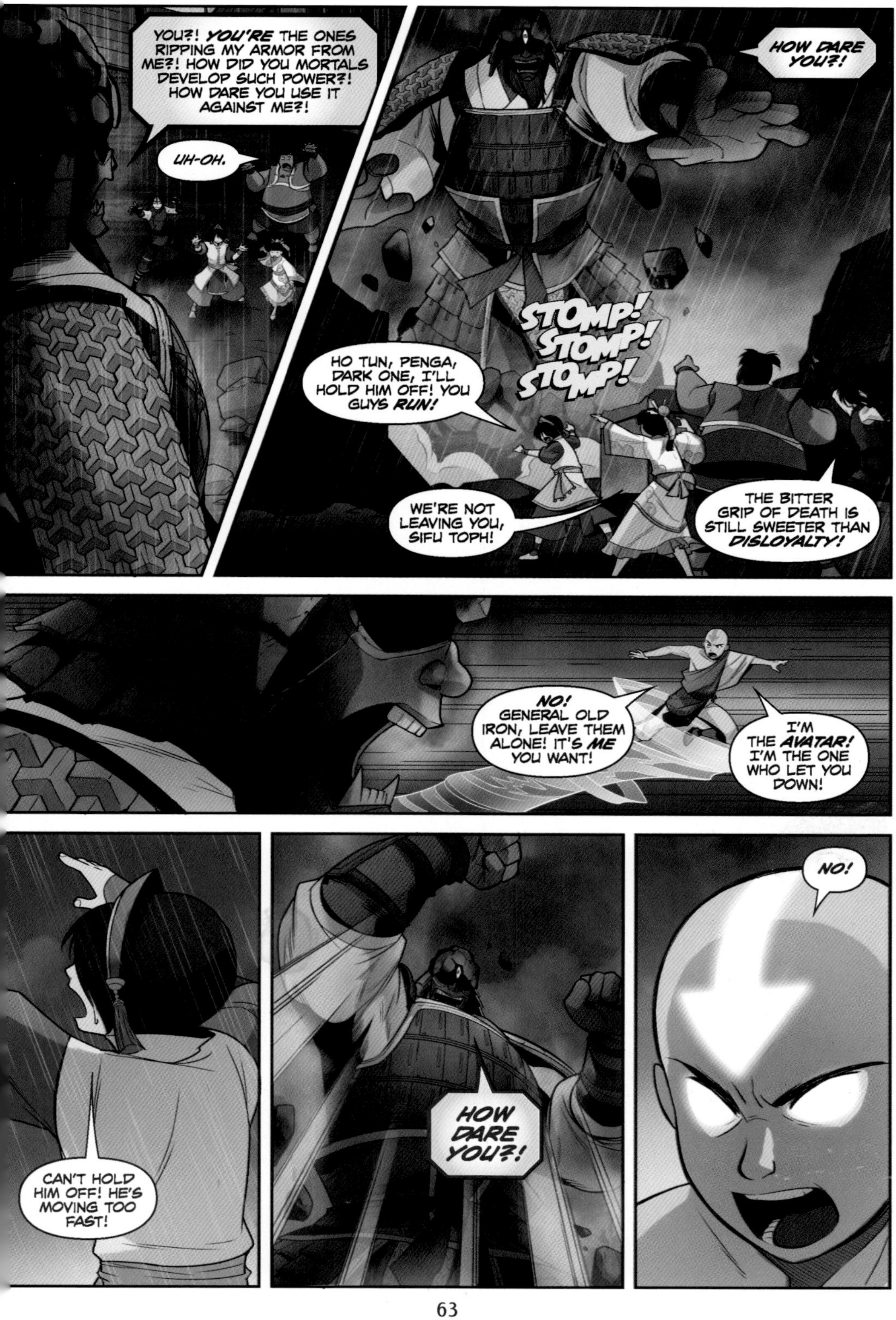
YOU?! YOU'RE THE ONES RIPPING MY ARMOR FROM ME?! HOW DID YOU MORTALS DEVELOP SUCH POWER?! HOW DARE YOU USE IT AGAINST ME?!
UH-OH.
HOW DARE YOU?!
STOMP! STOMP! STOMP!
HO TUN, PENGA, DARK ONE, I'LL HOLD HIM OFF! YOU GUYS RUN!
WE'RE NOT LEAVING YOU, SIFU TOPH!
THE BITTER GRIP OF DEATH IS STILL SWEETER THAN DISLOYALTY!
NO! GENERAL OLD IRON, LEAVE THEM ALONE! IT'S ME YOU WANT!
I'M THE AVATAR! I'M THE ONE WHO LET YOU DOWN!
CAN'T HOLD HIM OFF! HE'S MOVING TOO FAST!
HOW DARE YOU?!
NO!

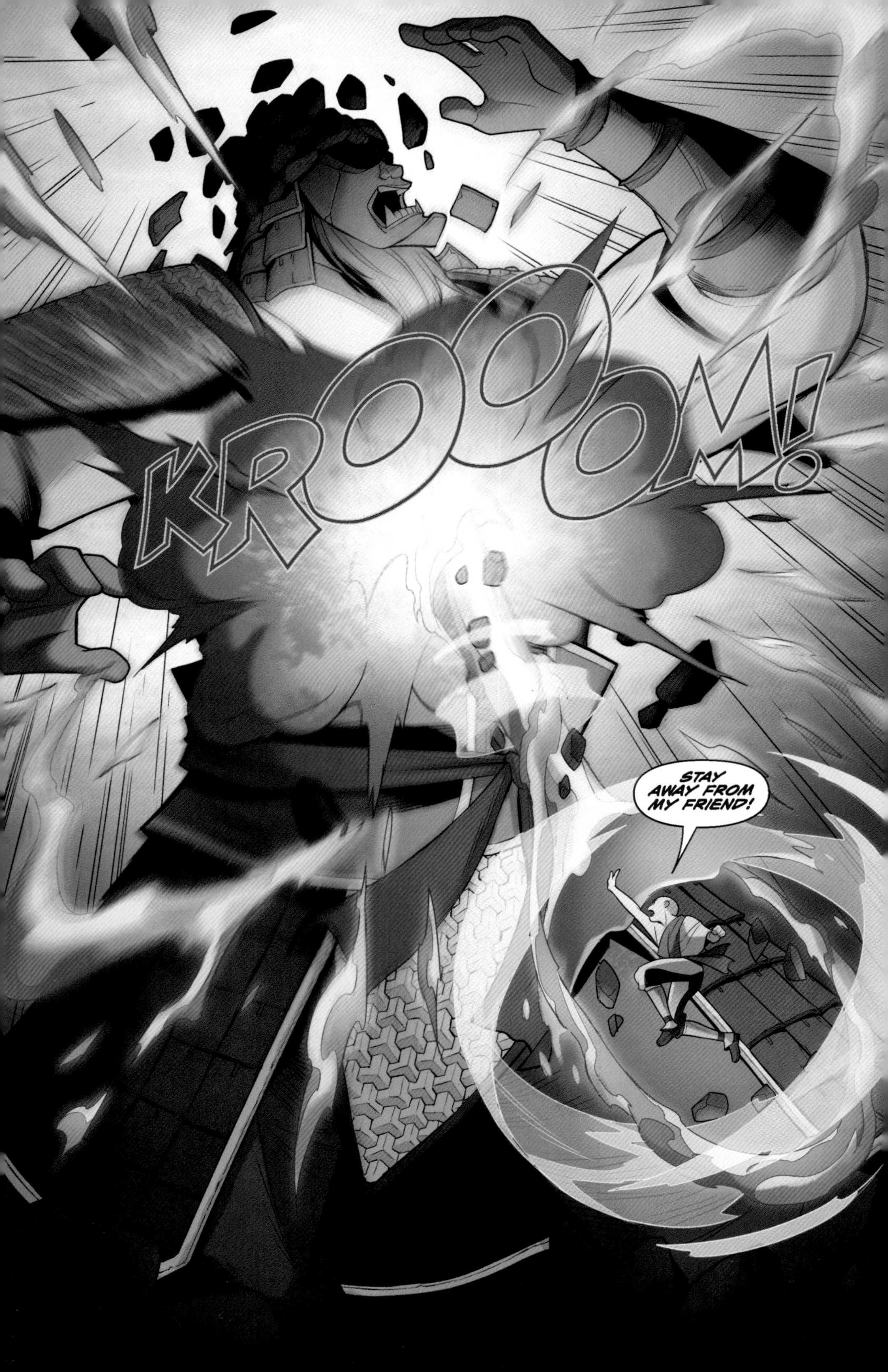
KROOOOM!
STAY AWAY FROM MY FRIEND!

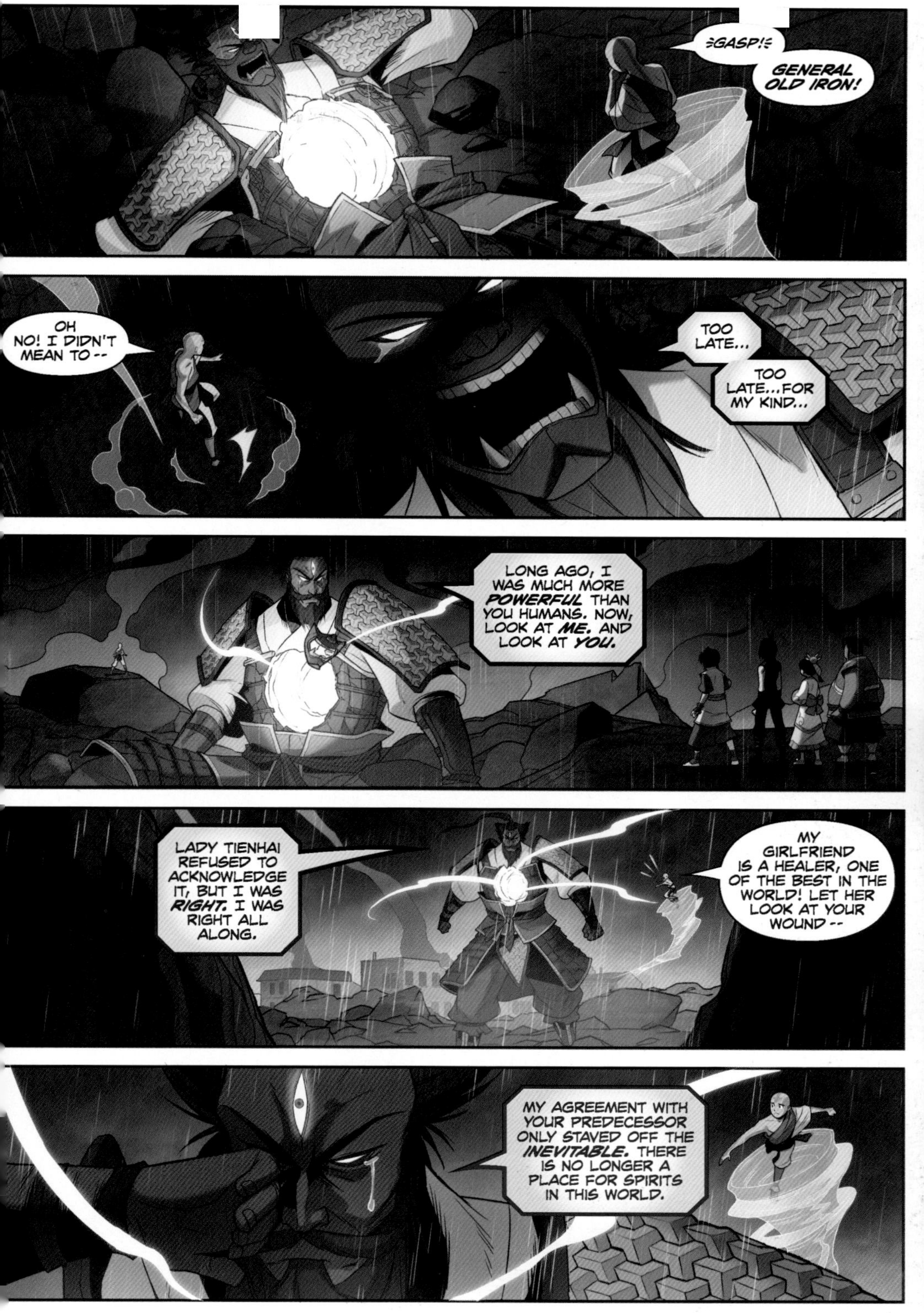

⸗GASP!⸗
GENERAL OLD IRON!
OH NO! I DIDN'T MEAN TO --
TOO LATE...
TOO LATE...FOR MY KIND...
LONG AGO, I WAS MUCH MORE POWERFUL THAN YOU HUMANS. NOW, LOOK AT ME. AND LOOK AT YOU.
LADY TIENHAI REFUSED TO ACKNOWLEDGE IT, BUT I WAS RIGHT. I WAS RIGHT ALL ALONG.
MY GIRLFRIEND IS A HEALER, ONE OF THE BEST IN THE WORLD! LET HER LOOK AT YOUR WOUND --
MY AGREEMENT WITH YOUR PREDECESSOR ONLY STAVED OFF THE INEVITABLE. THERE IS NO LONGER A PLACE FOR SPIRITS IN THIS WORLD.

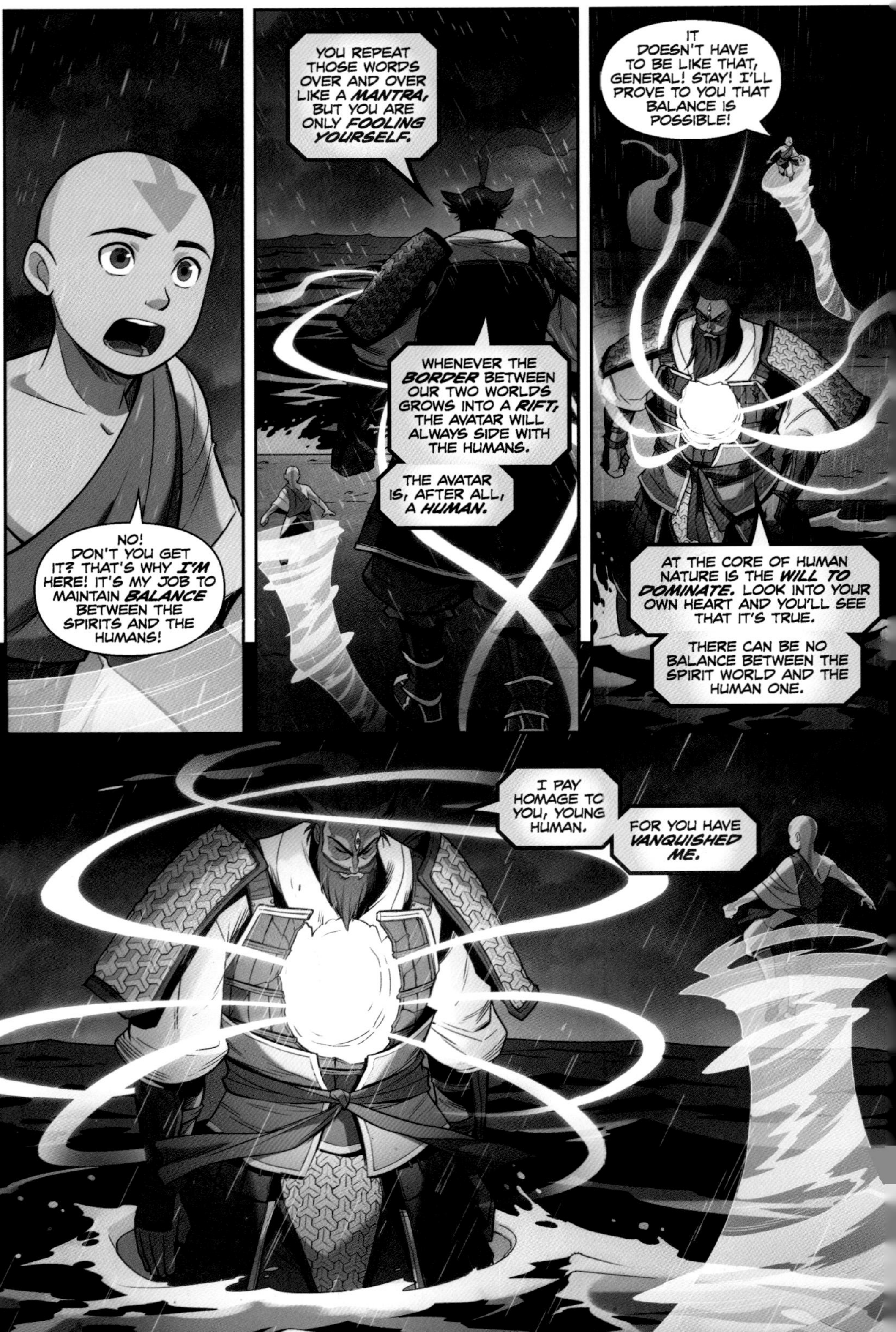
NO! DON'T YOU GET IT? THAT'S WHY I'M HERE! IT'S MY JOB TO MAINTAIN BALANCE BETWEEN THE SPIRITS AND THE HUMANS!
YOU REPEAT THOSE WORDS OVER AND OVER LIKE A MANTRA, BUT YOU ARE ONLY FOOLING YOURSELF.
WHENEVER THE BORDER BETWEEN OUR TWO WORLDS GROWS INTO A RIFT, THE AVATAR WILL ALWAYS SIDE WITH THE HUMANS.
THE AVATAR IS, AFTER ALL, A HUMAN.
IT DOESN'T HAVE TO BE LIKE THAT, GENERAL! STAY! I'LL PROVE TO YOU THAT BALANCE IS POSSIBLE!
AT THE CORE OF HUMAN NATURE IS THE WILL TO DOMINATE. LOOK INTO YOUR OWN HEART AND YOU'LL SEE THAT IT'S TRUE.
THERE CAN BE NO BALANCE BETWEEN THE SPIRIT WORLD AND THE HUMAN ONE.
I PAY HOMAGE TO YOU, YOUNG HUMAN.
FOR YOU HAVE VANQUISHED ME.

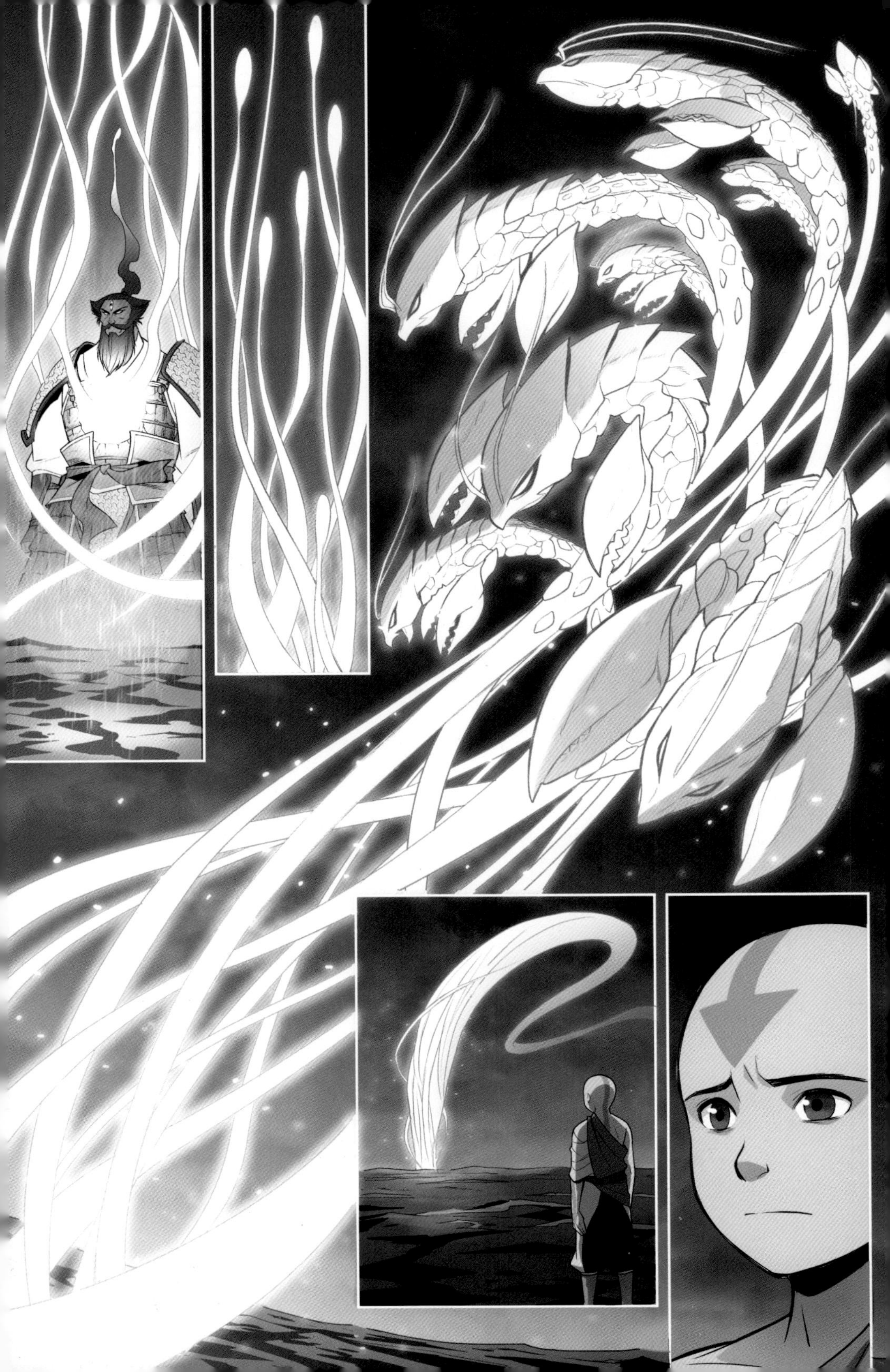

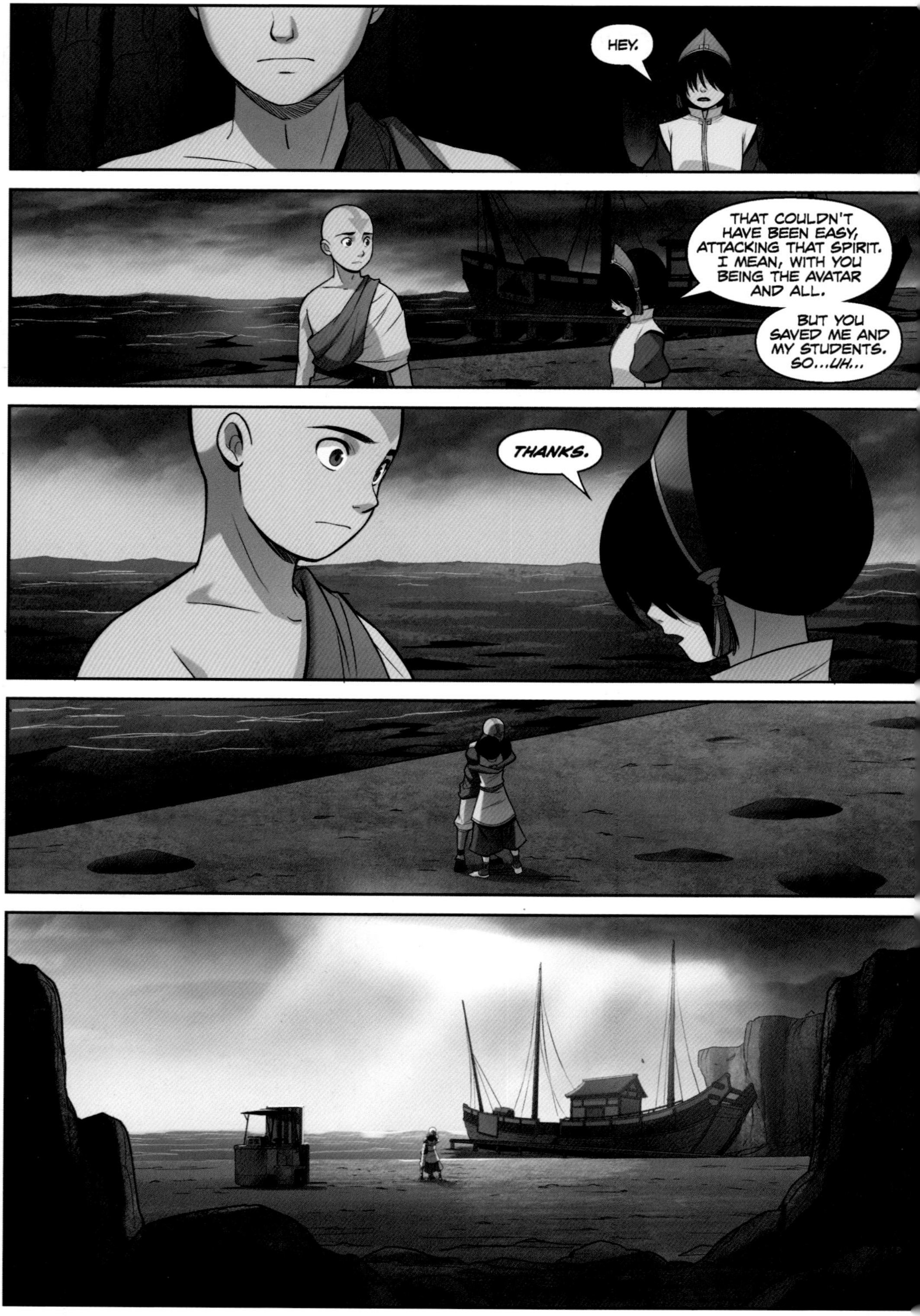
HEY.
THAT COULDN'T HAVE BEEN EASY, ATTACKING THAT SPIRIT. I MEAN, WITH YOU BEING THE AVATAR AND ALL.
BUT YOU SAVED ME AND MY STUDENTS. SO...UH...
THANKS.

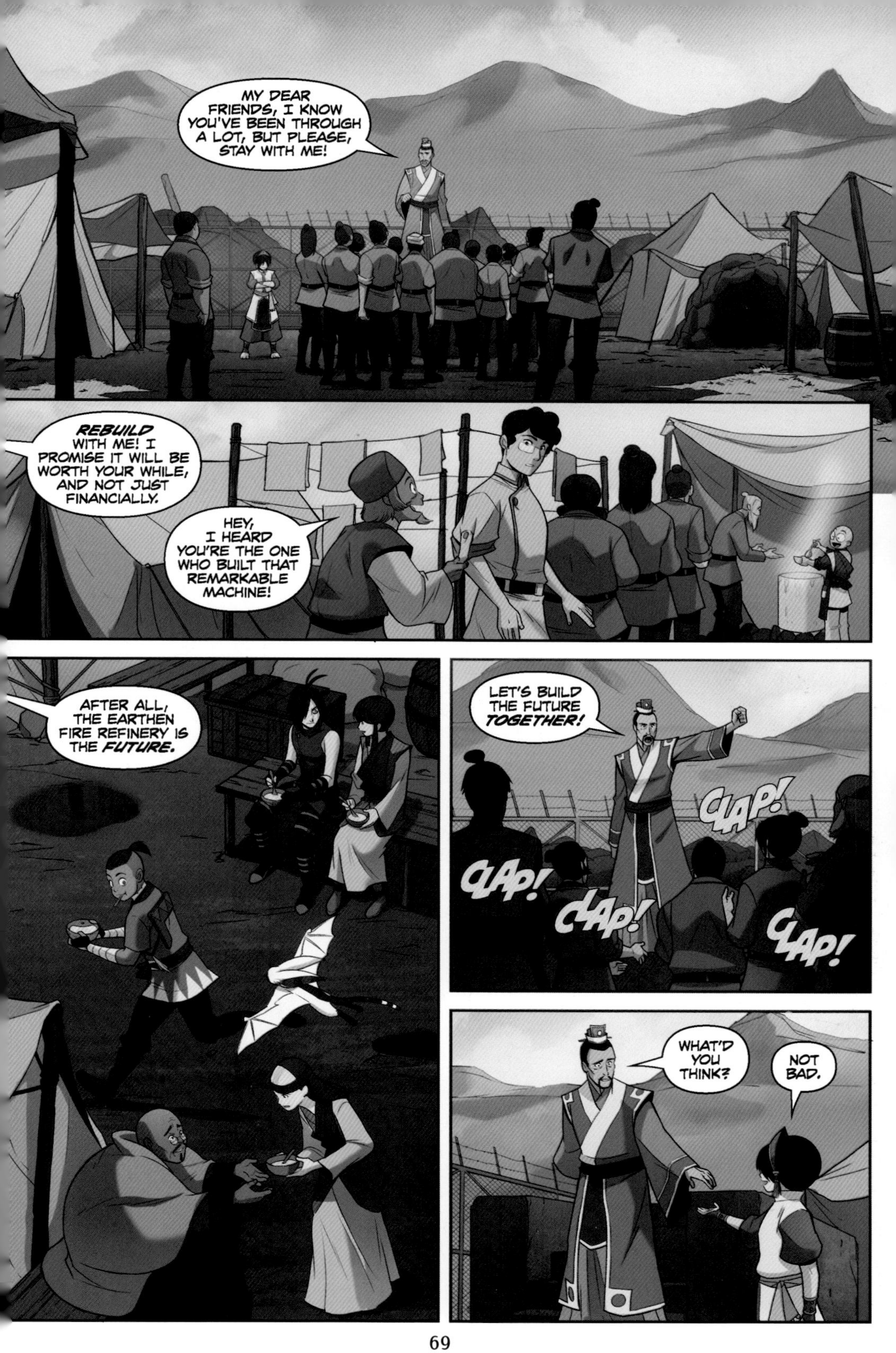
MY DEAR FRIENDS, I KNOW YOU'VE BEEN THROUGH A LOT, BUT PLEASE, STAY WITH ME!
REBUILD WITH ME! I PROMISE IT WILL BE WORTH YOUR WHILE, AND NOT JUST FINANCIALLY.
HEY, I HEARD YOU'RE THE ONE WHO BUILT THAT REMARKABLE MACHINE!
AFTER ALL, THE EARTHEN FIRE REFINERY IS THE *FUTURE.*
LET'S BUILD THE FUTURE *TOGETHER!*
CLAP!
CLAP!
CLAP!
CLAP!
WHAT'D YOU THINK?
NOT BAD.

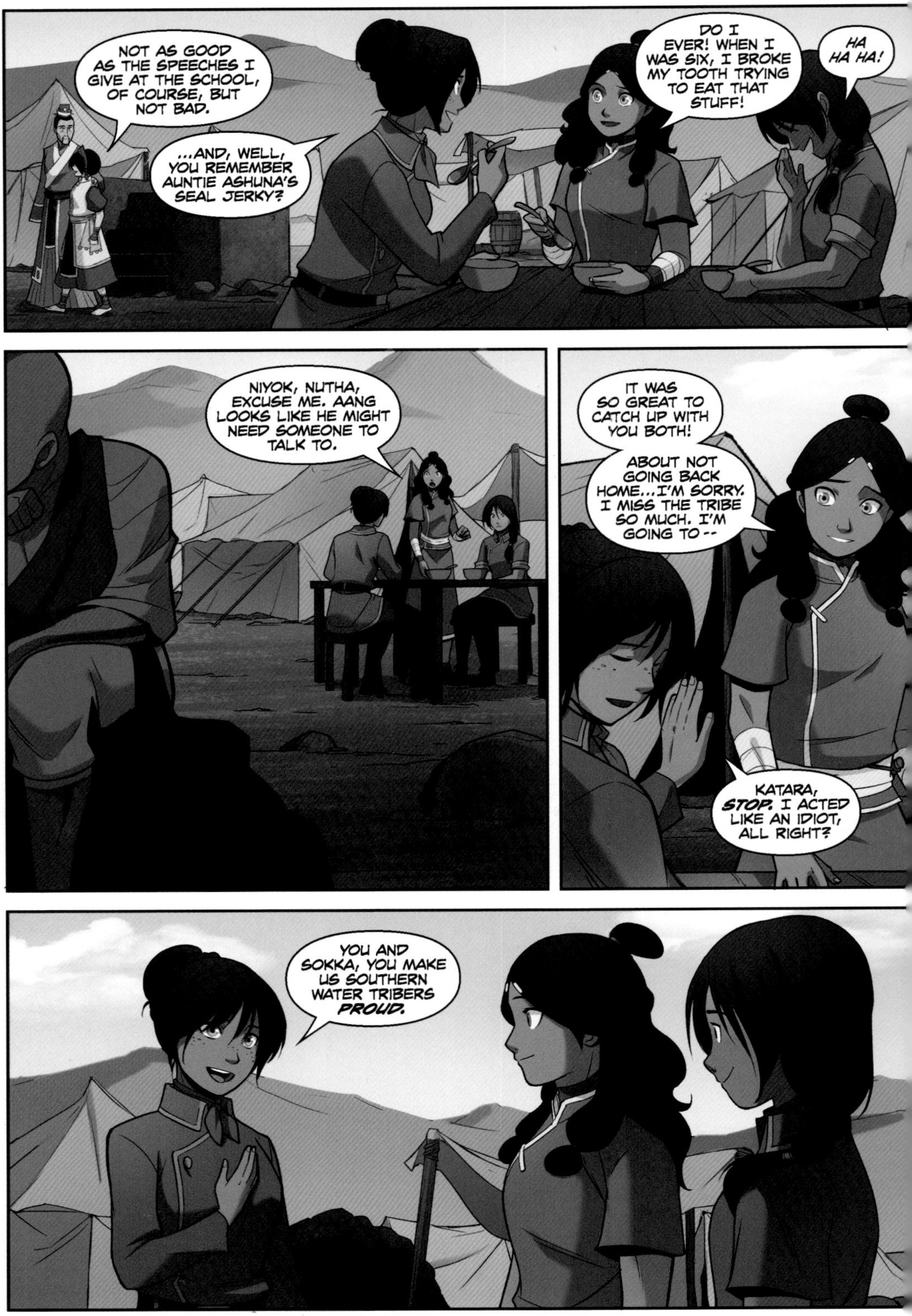
NOT AS GOOD AS THE SPEECHES I GIVE AT THE SCHOOL, OF COURSE, BUT NOT BAD.
...AND, WELL, YOU REMEMBER AUNTIE ASHUNA'S SEAL JERKY?
DO I EVER! WHEN I WAS SIX, I BROKE MY TOOTH TRYING TO EAT THAT STUFF!
HA HA HA!
NIYOK, NUTHA, EXCUSE ME. AANG LOOKS LIKE HE MIGHT NEED SOMEONE TO TALK TO.
IT WAS SO GREAT TO CATCH UP WITH YOU BOTH!
ABOUT NOT GOING BACK HOME...I'M SORRY. I MISS THE TRIBE SO MUCH. I'M GOING TO --
KATARA, *STOP.* I ACTED LIKE AN IDIOT, ALL RIGHT?
YOU AND SOKKA, YOU MAKE US SOUTHERN WATER TRIBERS *PROUD.*

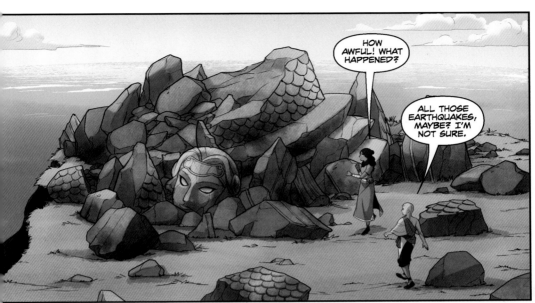

HOW AWFUL! WHAT HAPPENED?

ALL THOSE EARTHQUAKES, MAYBE? I'M NOT SURE.

GENERAL OLD IRON BELIEVED THAT THE SPIRITS NO LONGER HAVE A PLACE HERE. WHAT IF HE'S RIGHT?

WHAT IF THE SPIRITS ARE...ARE... JUST *RELICS* OF THE PAST, WITH NO *FUTURE* IN THE HUMAN WORLD?

THAT CAN'T BE TRUE, AANG.

I BELIEVE IN THE *AVATAR.* I BELIEVE IN *YOU.*

YOU'RE BETWEEN THE SPIRITS AND US. IF YOU HAVE A PART IN OUR WORLD'S FUTURE, THEN THE SPIRITS MUST HAVE ONE, TOO.

MAYBE YOU OUGHT TO TALK TO ONE OF YOUR PAST LIVES ABOUT IT.

I DON'T KNOW...WE'RE TALKING ABOUT THE *FUTURE,* AND THEY'RE MY *PAST* LIVES.

I DON'T THINK THE PAST AND THE FUTURE ARE *SEPARATE.* THEY'RE CONNECTED, YOU KNOW? BY *TODAY.* BY *US.*

FIND ME IF YOU NEED ME, SWEETIE.

I WILL.

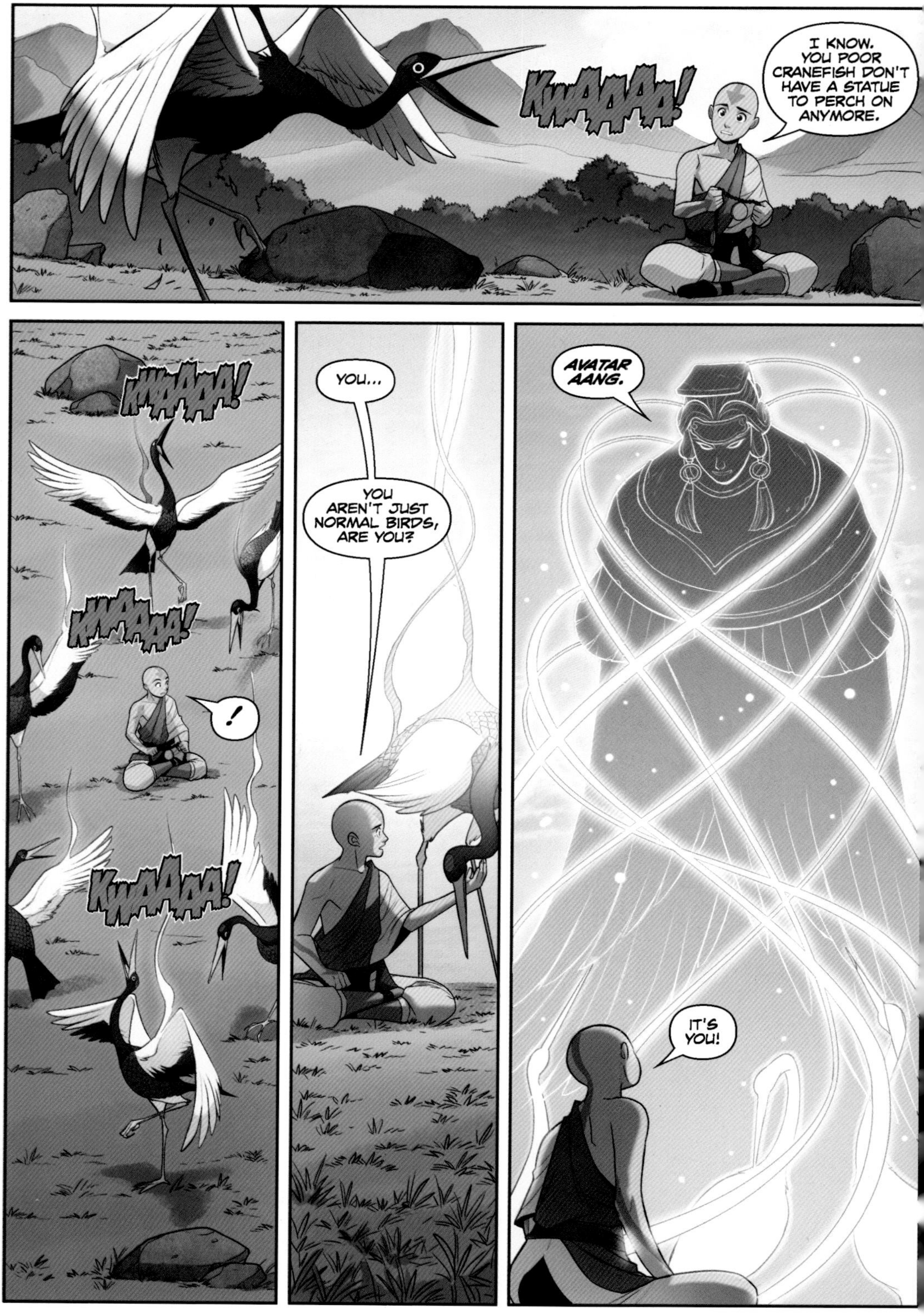
KWAAAAA!
I KNOW. YOU POOR CRANEFISH DON'T HAVE A STATUE TO PERCH ON ANYMORE.
KWAAAA!
KWAAAA!
!
KWAAAA!
YOU...
YOU AREN'T JUST NORMAL BIRDS, ARE YOU?
AVATAR AANG.
IT'S YOU!

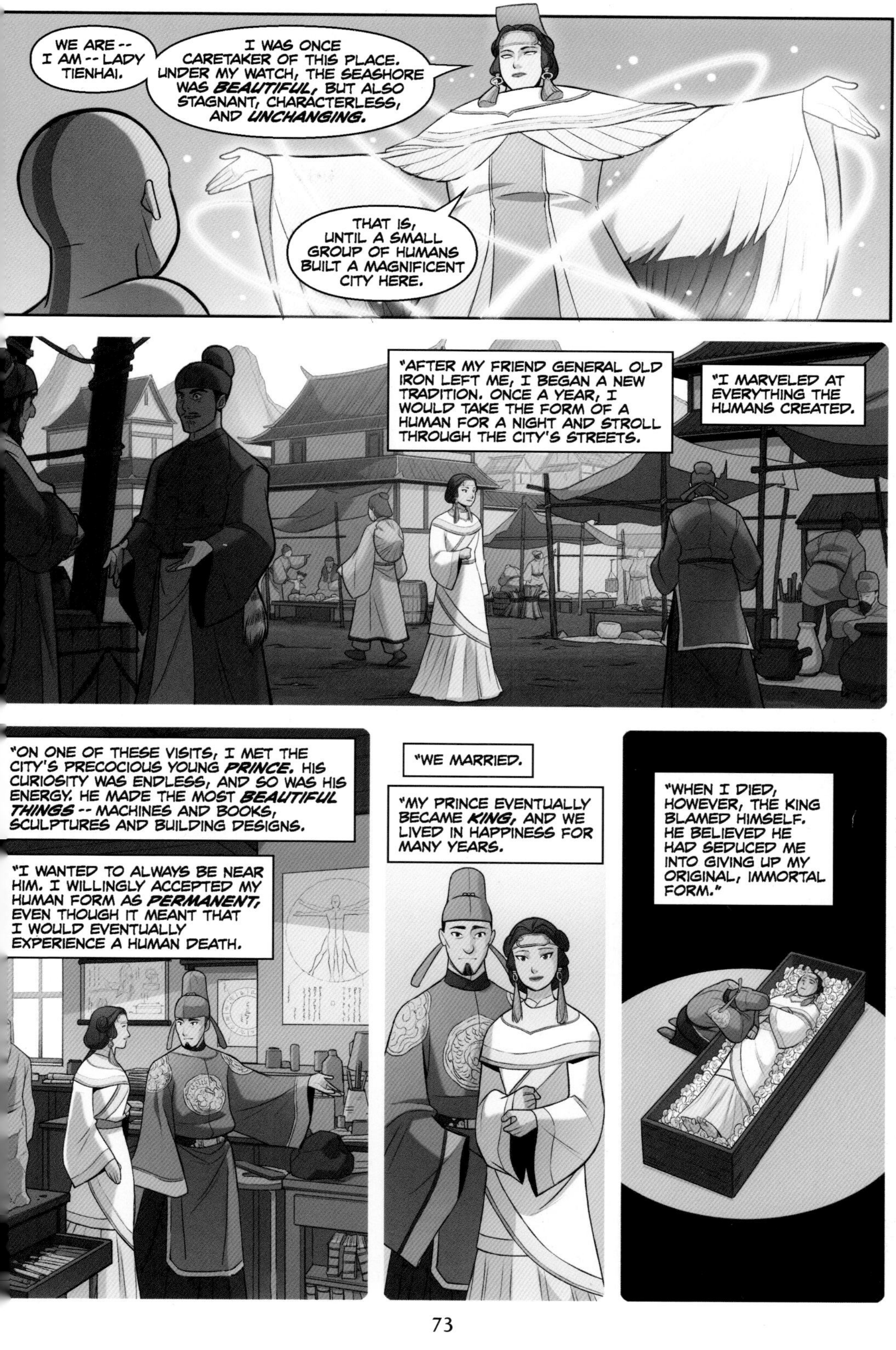
WE ARE -- I AM -- LADY TIENHAI.
I WAS ONCE CARETAKER OF THIS PLACE. UNDER MY WATCH, THE SEASHORE WAS BEAUTIFUL, BUT ALSO STAGNANT, CHARACTERLESS, AND UNCHANGING.
THAT IS, UNTIL A SMALL GROUP OF HUMANS BUILT A MAGNIFICENT CITY HERE.
"AFTER MY FRIEND GENERAL OLD IRON LEFT ME, I BEGAN A NEW TRADITION. ONCE A YEAR, I WOULD TAKE THE FORM OF A HUMAN FOR A NIGHT AND STROLL THROUGH THE CITY'S STREETS.
"I MARVELED AT EVERYTHING THE HUMANS CREATED.
"ON ONE OF THESE VISITS, I MET THE CITY'S PRECOCIOUS YOUNG PRINCE. HIS CURIOSITY WAS ENDLESS, AND SO WAS HIS ENERGY. HE MADE THE MOST BEAUTIFUL THINGS -- MACHINES AND BOOKS, SCULPTURES AND BUILDING DESIGNS.
"I WANTED TO ALWAYS BE NEAR HIM. I WILLINGLY ACCEPTED MY HUMAN FORM AS PERMANENT, EVEN THOUGH IT MEANT THAT I WOULD EVENTUALLY EXPERIENCE A HUMAN DEATH.
"WE MARRIED.
"MY PRINCE EVENTUALLY BECAME KING, AND WE LIVED IN HAPPINESS FOR MANY YEARS.
"WHEN I DIED, HOWEVER, THE KING BLAMED HIMSELF. HE BELIEVED HE HAD SEDUCED ME INTO GIVING UP MY ORIGINAL, IMMORTAL FORM."

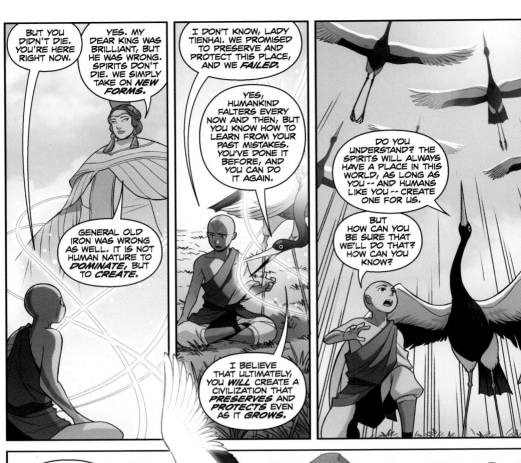

BUT YOU DIDN'T DIE. YOU'RE HERE RIGHT NOW.

YES, MY DEAR KING WAS BRILLIANT, BUT HE WAS WRONG. SPIRITS DON'T DIE. WE SIMPLY TAKE ON *NEW FORMS.*

GENERAL OLD IRON WAS WRONG AS WELL. IT IS NOT HUMAN NATURE TO *DOMINATE,* BUT TO *CREATE.*

I DON'T KNOW, LADY TIENHAI. WE PROMISED TO PRESERVE AND PROTECT THIS PLACE, AND WE *FAILED.*

YES, HUMANKIND FALTERS EVERY NOW AND THEN, BUT YOU KNOW HOW TO LEARN FROM YOUR PAST MISTAKES. YOU'VE DONE IT BEFORE, AND YOU CAN DO IT AGAIN.

I BELIEVE THAT ULTIMATELY, YOU *WILL* CREATE A CIVILIZATION THAT *PRESERVES* AND *PROTECTS* EVEN AS IT *GROWS.*

DO YOU UNDERSTAND? THE SPIRITS WILL ALWAYS HAVE A PLACE IN THIS WORLD, AS LONG AS YOU -- AND HUMANS LIKE YOU -- CREATE ONE FOR US.

BUT HOW CAN YOU BE SURE THAT WE'LL DO THAT? HOW CAN YOU KNOW?

I DON'T KNOW, YOUNG AVATAR. I *HOPE.*

KwAAAa!

KwAAAa!

KwAAAa!

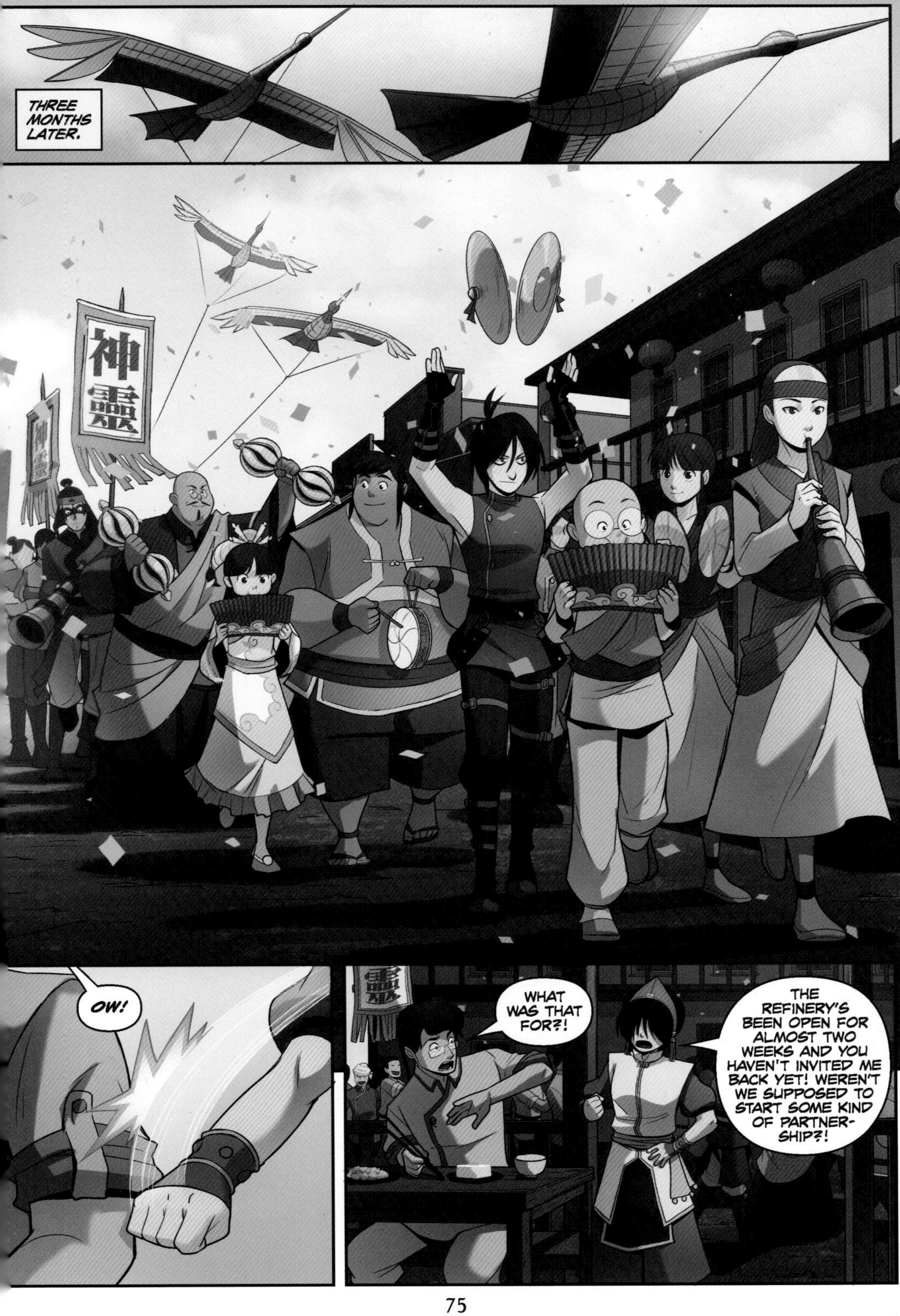
THREE MONTHS LATER.
神靈
OW!
WHAT WAS THAT FOR?!
THE REFINERY'S BEEN OPEN FOR ALMOST TWO WEEKS AND YOU HAVEN'T INVITED ME BACK YET! WEREN'T WE SUPPOSED TO START SOME KIND OF PARTNER-SHIP?!

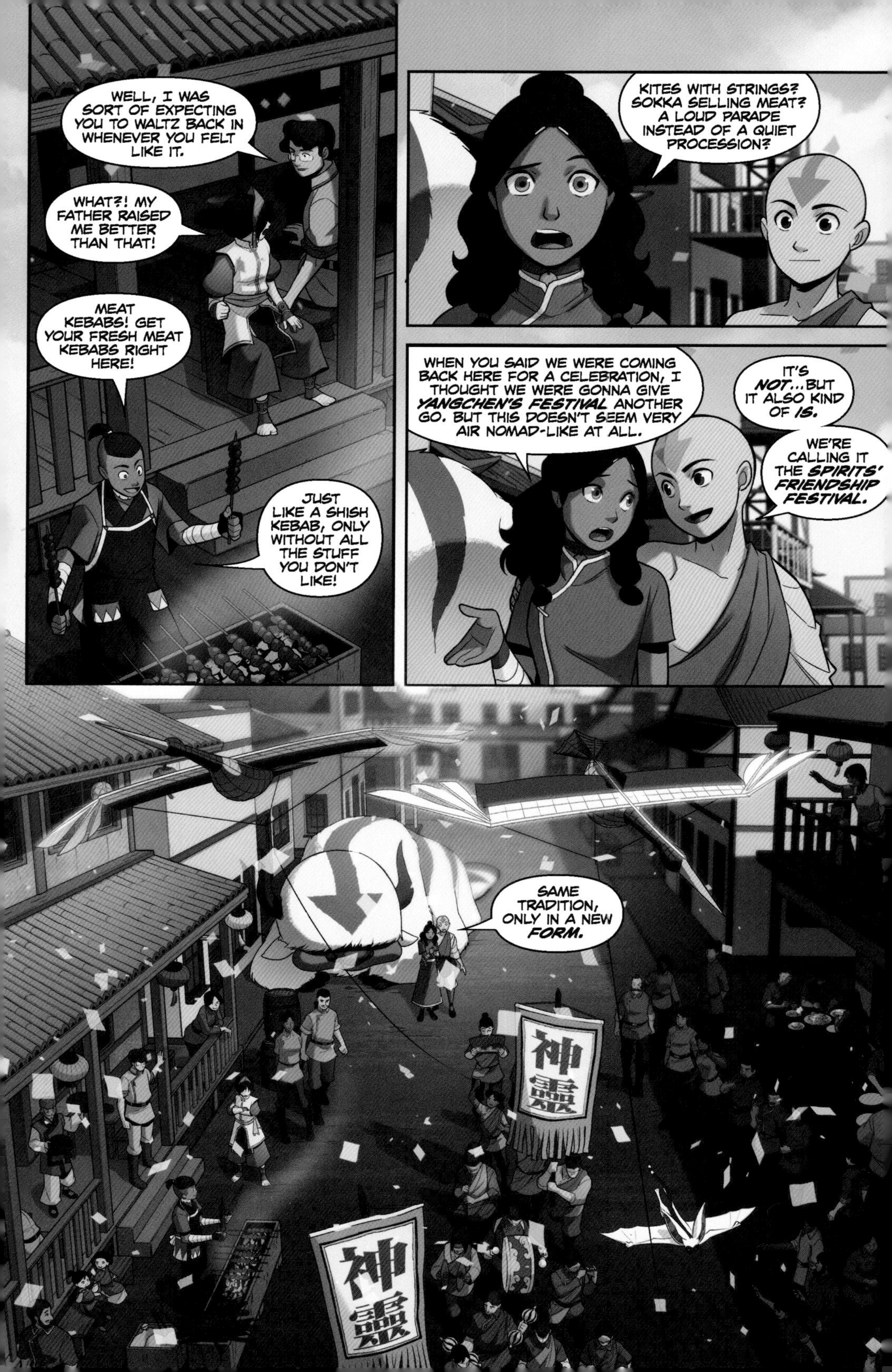
WELL, I WAS SORT OF EXPECTING YOU TO WALTZ BACK IN WHENEVER YOU FELT LIKE IT.
WHAT?! MY FATHER RAISED ME BETTER THAN THAT!
MEAT KEBABS! GET YOUR FRESH MEAT KEBABS RIGHT HERE!
JUST LIKE A SHISH KEBAB, ONLY WITHOUT ALL THE STUFF YOU DON'T LIKE!
KITES WITH STRINGS? SOKKA SELLING MEAT? A LOUD PARADE INSTEAD OF A QUIET PROCESSION?
WHEN YOU SAID WE WERE COMING BACK HERE FOR A CELEBRATION, I THOUGHT WE WERE GONNA GIVE YANGCHEN'S FESTIVAL ANOTHER GO. BUT THIS DOESN'T SEEM VERY AIR NOMAD-LIKE AT ALL.
IT'S NOT...BUT IT ALSO KIND OF IS.
WE'RE CALLING IT THE SPIRITS' FRIENDSHIP FESTIVAL.
SAME TRADITION, ONLY IN A NEW FORM.
神靈
神靈

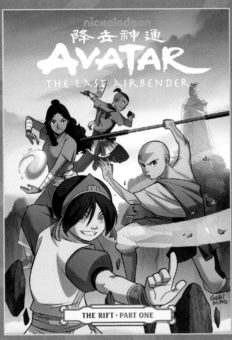
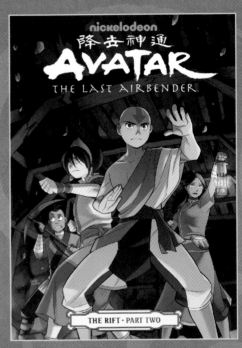

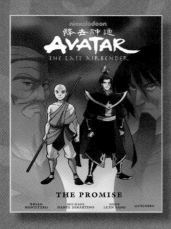

Avatar: The Last Airbender—The Promise Library Edition
978-1-61655-074-5 $39.99

Avatar: The Last Airbender—The Promise Part 1
978-1-59582-811-8 $10.99

Avatar: The Last Airbender—The Promise Part 2
978-1-59582-875-0 $10.99

Avatar: The Last Airbender—The Promise Part 3
978-1-59582-941-2 $10.99

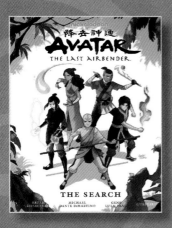

Avatar: The Last Airbender—The Search Library Edition
978-1-61655-226-8 $39.99

Avatar: The Last Airbender—The Search Part 1
978-1-61655-054-7 $10.99

Avatar: The Last Airbender—The Search Part 2
978-1-61655-190-2 $10.99

Avatar: The Last Airbender—The Search Part 3
978-1-61655-184-1 $10.99

Avatar: The Last Airbender—The Art of the Animated Series
978-1-59582-504-9 $34.99

Avatar: The Last Airbender—The Lost Adventures
978-1-59582-748-7 $14.99

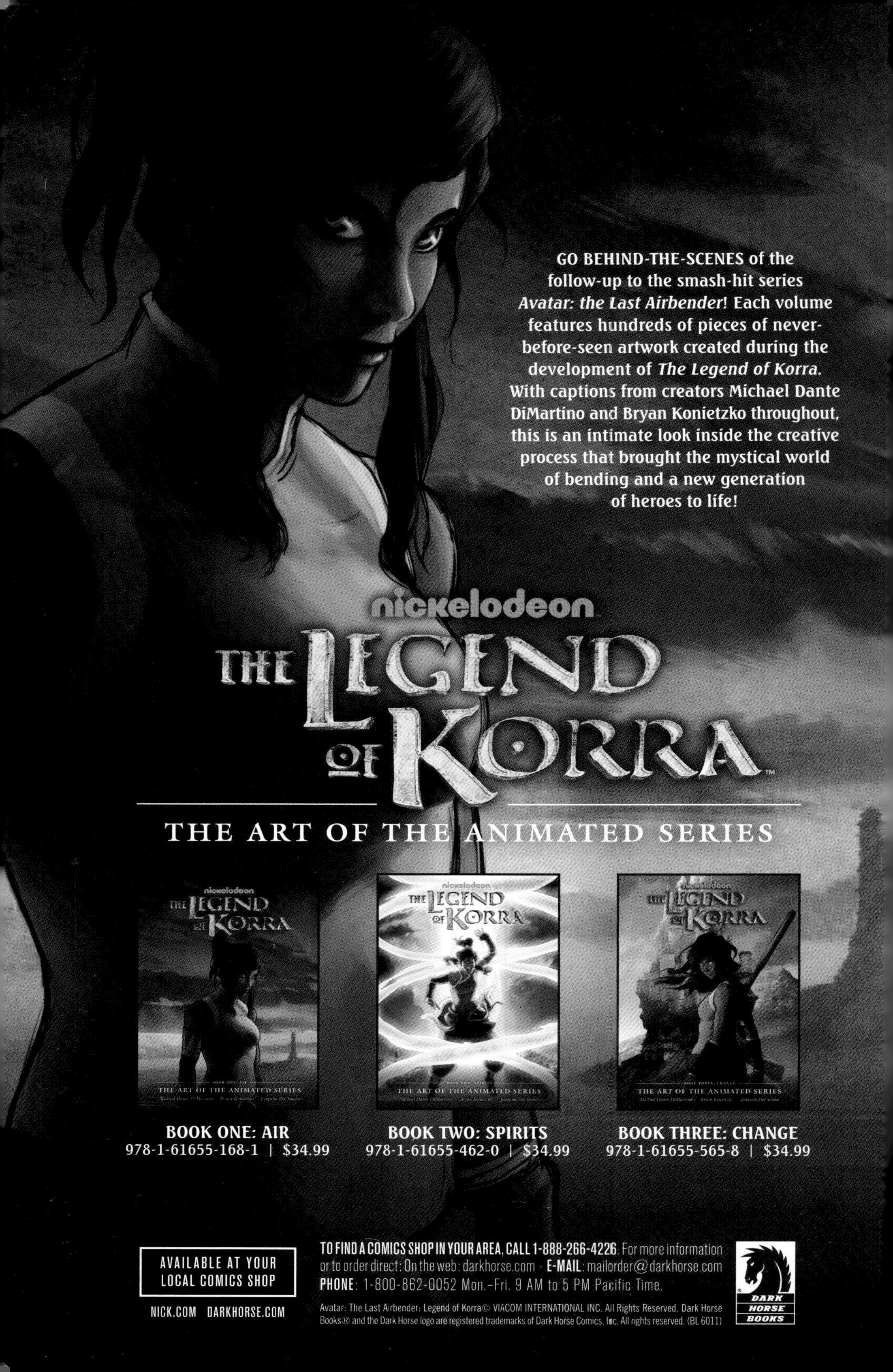
GO BEHIND-THE-SCENES of the follow-up to the smash-hit series *Avatar: the Last Airbender*! Each volume features hundreds of pieces of never-before-seen artwork created during the development of *The Legend of Korra.* With captions from creators Michael Dante DiMartino and Bryan Konietzko throughout, this is an intimate look inside the creative process that brought the mystical world of bending and a new generation of heroes to life!
nickelodeon
THE LEGEND OF KORRA™
THE ART OF THE ANIMATED SERIES
nickelodeon
THE LEGEND OF KORRA
THE ART OF THE ANIMATED SERIES
nickelodeon
THE LEGEND OF KORRA
THE ART OF THE ANIMATED SERIES
nickelodeon
THE LEGEND OF KORRA
THE ART OF THE ANIMATED SERIES
BOOK ONE: AIR
978-1-61655-168-1 | $34.99
BOOK TWO: SPIRITS
978-1-61655-462-0 | $34.99
BOOK THREE: CHANGE
978-1-61655-565-8 | $34.99
AVAILABLE AT YOUR LOCAL COMICS SHOP
NICK.COM DARKHORSE.COM
TO FIND A COMICS SHOP IN YOUR AREA, CALL 1-888-266-4226. For more information or to order direct: On the web: darkhorse.com · E-MAIL: mailorder@darkhorse.com
PHONE: 1-800-862-0052 Mon.–Fri. 9 AM to 5 PM Pacific Time.
Avatar: The Last Airbender: Legend of Korra© VIACOM INTERNATIONAL INC. All Rights Reserved. Dark Horse Books® and the Dark Horse logo are registered trademarks of Dark Horse Comics, Inc. All rights reserved. (BL 6011)
DARK HORSE BOOKS